CHILD LABOUR IN HOME BASED SECTOR

By

Dr. A. Selva Kumar

M.Com., M.Phil., M.B.A., Ph.D.
Reader
Department of Commerce, Pope's College
Sawyarpuram-628 251
Tuticorin, District Tamil Nadu

SONALI PUBLICATIONS
New Delhi-110002

Edition-2019

ISBN: 81-88836-68-0

Published By

SONALI PUBLICATIONS
4228/1, Ansari Road, Darya Ganj,
New Delhi - 110 002 (India)
Ph.: 011-23266109
Fax : 91-011-23283267
e-mail-sonalipub@yahoo.co.in

Printed at:
Sachin Printers, Delhi-53

Contents

Foreword

An ugly face of Indian economy is the widespread unemployment with the resultant poverty especially in the countryside. Of late, some notable achievements have been made in the economic field, particularly in the industrial sphere.

Unemployment occurs in various forms, depending on the level of economic growth. At the lower level of development, with backward agriculture predominant, unemployment takes two forms, namely, disguised unemployment and seasonal unemployment. Against this background, child labour is prevailing throughout the country. The present research book entitled "Child Labour in Home Based Sector" is based on the author's earlier Ph.D., thesis captioned "A Study on Child Labour in Beedi Industry in Tirunelveli District in Tamil Nadu State" the thesis submitted under the supervision of Dr.R.Neelamegam, the then Professor and Head of the Department of Corporate Secretaryship, Alagappa University, Karaikudi, Tamil Nadu; as well as under the Co-Supervision of Dr.G.Karunanithi, Professor and Head, Department of Sociology, Manonmaniam Sundaranar University, Tirunelveli, Tamil Nadu.

The book is first of its kind in the field in giving a detailed account on employment of child workers in Tirunelveli District. This trend has to be reversed and full employment at continuously rising income has to be ensured if the present economic growth is to be really meaningful for the vast masses. A notable feature is the researcher's incorporation of practical suggestions to tackle the problem of employment of child labour.

I congratulate Dr.A.Selvakumar for brining out in this edition the latest developments in the field. He has dealt not only with the narrative part of the practices of child labour but also tired to critically evaluate them in the context of business in India.

I am quite sure that the book would be highly useful to those who are interested in child labour. It is a pleasure to record overtly my appreciation to the Discovery Publishing House, New Delhi. Who so intelligently assumed the much demanding task of preparing the Ph.D., thesis for publication.

Dr. RAM NEELAMEGAM
Professor and Head (Retd.)
Department of Corporate Secretaryship
Alagappa University
Karaikudi - 630003
Tamil Nadu.

Preface

Child Labour is a universal phenomenon. Its prevalence is seen almost in all periods of time. Until recently, few attempts have been made to understand its genesis and processes. However, it is the declaration of the year 1979 as the International Year of the Child by the United Nations which has exposed the magnitude of the problem in its varied dimensions. The problem of child labour is rooted in the socio-economic conditions prevailing in a country. Children work under unsuitable conditions that are detrimental to their health and development. Employment of children at an early age hampers their mental, physical and psychological growth. This in turn affects severely the socio-economic and cultural growth of any country unleashing the problem of child labour.

Child labour as a social problem has become an important component of welfare consciousness among the public, social organisations and the State. The problem of child labour is mankind's belated recognition that children are important, and that care for each stage of a child's growth is imperative if a nation is to prosper. In the present study, an attempt has been made to find out the socio-economic factors which play a significant role in pushing children into the labour force and the repercussions of early employment. The study discloses that poverty, indebtedness, social customs and attitude of parents to education are the main reasons which forced children to work as labourers.

India is not able to tackle the problem of child labour even after 58 years of Independence. Inspite of a tremendous scientific and technological advancement that India is registering every year, millions of children in the country are denied the right to education and lead a life of dignity.

A great majority of the of girl children are employed by their parents to roll beedis to roll beedis in domestic settings. The reason is that the girl children are considered as liability to the parents. They are not only deprived of their education and recreation, but they are subject to gender discrimination at their homes and risks of sexual harassment at their work place outside home.

This study highlights how the child labour in home based beediworks are deprived of their education and other childhood activities. Further, it provides a detailed explanation of their working and living conditions, exploitation, harassment, denial of basic rights, health hazards and legal interventions. It recommends that government should enforce compulsory primary education to check the problem of child labour and also insists that the parents should be prepared for sacrifice their life for the betterment of their children.

At the outset I offer my prayer to the God, Almighty who showered His blessings on me to execute this work. But for His Grace this humble piece of work would not have been presented in this form.

I am extremely thankful to Dr. Ram Neelamegam, Former Professor and Head, Department of Corporate Secretaryship, Alagappa University, Karaikudi, Tamilnadu, for having consented to write a foreword for this book. His useful comments and suggestions helped me immensely to bring this book.

I express my gratitude to Dr. G.Karunanithi, Professor and Head, Department of Sociology, Manonmaniam Sundaranar University, Tirunelveli, Tamil Nadu, for his suggestions and help to publish this work.

My sincere thanks to The Rt. Rev. Dr. S.Jeyapaul David, Bishop of Tirunelveli Diocese, Tirunelveli, Tamil Nadu, and Mrs.Violet Jeyapaul for their constant encouragement and prayer support to complete the publication work.

I am thankful to Rev. J.S.Anand Asir, and Rev. Mrs. Jessie Anand, Leister, United Kingdom for their kind inspiration and prayer support.

I also thank Mr. J.J.Gurusingh and Mrs. Kanaga Gurusingh, 'MISBA', Sawyerpuram for their prayer support and encouragement all throughout.

I thank Dr. J.Balasingh, Former Principal, St. John's College, Palayamkottai, Tirunelveli and now Director, P.S.N.College of Engineering and Technology, Tirunelvlei for his timely help for this research work.

I thank Dr. C.Kumar Charlie Paul, Principal, Francis Xavier Engineering College, Tirunelveli for his kind encouragement.

I would like to place on record my special thanks to my friends Mr. D.Jeyasingh, Selection Grade Lecturer in Economics, Pope's College, Mr. J.Jeyasingh, Selection Grade Lecturer in Economics, Pope's College and Mr. M.A.Mohamed Samsudeen, P.G. Assistant in English, Muslim Higher Secondary School, Abiramam, Mr. S.M.A.Syed Mohamed Khaja, Manager, Sadakathullah Appa College, Palayamkottai, and my colleagues for their kind encouragement to bringout this book.

I express my sincere thanks to the respondents who extend cooperation and provided pertinent information during my field work for this study.

I avail myself of this opportunity to express my deep sense of gratitude to my beloved parents, Mr. D.Ayyapillai and Mrs.Mariammal, in-laws Mr. N.Francis, Mrs. Leela Francis and Mr. F. Suresh Jesuwin and my elder brother Dr. A.Arul Devadoss, Reader in History, St. John's College, Palayamkottai for all their moral and material support. My dear wife Mrs. Graceline Julia Selvakumar, daughters Selvi.S.Letishia Mary and Baby S.Ida Blessy were three silent and prayerful upholders to me to publish this book.

I am very much thankful to the Discovery Publishing House, New Delhi, for taking sincere efforts to publish this book.

Last but not least, I thank Mr. M.A.Mohamed Younoos for his help in Computer typing work.

A. SELVA KUMAR

Acknowledgements

My grateful acknowledgement are due to the leading personalities for rendering valuable assistance for the successful completion of the present research report.

I convey my deep debt of gratitude to my research supervisor Dr. R. Neelamegam, Professor and Head, Department of Corporate Secretaryship, Alagappa University, Karaikudi, for his invaluable and meritorious research guidance and supervision. Indeed, it is my rare privilege to do research under Dr. R. Neelamegam. I find to exact word to convey my sincere thanks adequately to him for all the trouble he has undertaken since the onset of this research study. I have learnt from him how discipline, assiduity and earnestness go a long way in moulding the personality of a scholar. I overtly salute my supervisor for the completion of the present doctoral thesis in time.

I am greatly indebted to my co-guide Dr. G. Karunanithi, Reader in Sociology, Mononmaniam Sundaranar University, Tirunelveli, for his inspiring and scholarly guidance during the course of my research. It has been a pleasure and privilege to work under his supervision. Inspite of his pre-occupation with several academic responsibilities and assignments, he is kind enough to spare his valuable time for giving me the necessary counsel and guidance. The credit goes to my co-guide for presenting the data through textual, tabular and diagrammatic means. I have no words to express my gratitude to him. It is, indeed, his help, guidance and encouragement which have helped me to accomplish this work and I owe him whatever merit it has.

Officer, New Delhi, Mr. S. Durairaj, Sub Divisional Engineer-Telecom, Triunelveli and Mrs. Revathi Vishwanathan, ICSSR office, New Delhi in availing of this fellowship on time

I express my sincere thanks to All India Association for Christian Higher Education, for having accepted to extend financial support to complete my research work.

I extend my hearty thanks to my Department colleagues Mr. Aruldoss Henry Semuel, Head of the Department, Mr. A. Gnanadoss, Senior Scale Lecturer, Mr. J. Arulraj Deniel, Senior Scale Lecturer, Mr. J. Asir Thiyagarajan, Senior Scale Lecturer and Mr. T. Stanly, Lecturer, for the interest shown by them in the progress of the research work at various stages and their encouragement all throughout.

I would like to convey my thanks to Mr. B. Nala Chandrasekaran, Director, Navajeevan Trust, Zion Nagar, Tirunelveli, for his valuable help and solid support extended to me during the period of research.

I am also thankful to Mrs. G. Radha, Co-ordinator, Navajeevan Trust, Alangulam, Mr. A. Britto, Kavoor Chattram and Mr. S.A. Senthil Kannan, Melapalayam for their remarkable assistance and support during the collection of data required for my study.

I must express my sincere thanks to the respondents who supplied information in response to the interview-schedule, without their co-operation and help the field survey would not have been successful.

I heartily thank Dr. Mrs. Ida P. Joseph, Selection Grade Lecturer in English, Sarah-Tucker College, Palayamkottai, Dr. N. Poovalingam, Lecturer in English, Manonmaniam Sundaranar University and Mr. S. Mohamed Sherif, Selection Grade Lecturer in English, Sadakathullah Appa College, for their assistance extended to at various stages of my research work. They have made in precious comments and offered valuable suggestions for the successful completion of my study in time.

I am grateful to the Rt. Rev. Jason S. Dharmaraj, Bishop in Triunelveli Diocese and Chairman, TDTA Colleges Governing Board, for having appointed me as a Lecturer in 1987 at Pope's College, Sawyerpuram, the institution of high repute. I thank him a lot for his encouragement in doing the doctoral work.

I express my profound sense of gratitude to Major T.J.T. Rejkumar, Principal and Secretary, Pope's College, Sawyerpuram for graciously permitting me to carry on research work in the subject of Commerce and for his support and active help in the successful completion of my research work.

I wish to express my gratitude to Dr. J. Balasingh, Principal and Secretary, St. John's College, Palayamkottai for his unsagging encouragement and his timely help for the successful completion of the present research work.

I am extremely thankful to Prof. G. Mohamed Pasi, Formerly principal, Sadakathullah Appa College, Palayamkottai for his constant encouragement and the help rendered to me with whom I had fruitful discussion during the initial stages of my work.

I convey my deep sense of gratitude to the than Vice Chancellor and other officials of Alagappa University, Karaikudi for Permitting me to carry on my research work in the Department of Corporate Secretaryship, Alagappa University under the ICSSR's Partial Assistance Fellowship in the year 1997.

I heartily thank the faculty members of the Department of Corporate Secretaryship, Alagappa University for their encouragement all throughout.

I am thankful to the Indian Council of Social Science Research, New Delhi, for having provided me the "Partial Assistance Fellowship" which, indeed, enabled me to elaborate my work as I planned originally. I wish to acknowledge the timely help rendered to me by Mr. P. Paulraj, Junior Telecom

I am thankful to Dr. A. Loganathan, Lecturer in Statistics, Mononmaniam Sundaranar University, for his kind help to prepare necessary diagrams for the present thesis.

I am thankful to my friend Mr. A. Paul Pandi, Senior Superintendent, Manonmaniam Sundaranar University for this kind encouragement and timely help all throughout.

I would like to place on record my special thanks to Rev. J. Anand Asir and Mrs. Jessie Anand, Mr. M. John Vincent, Ex. M.L.A and my friends Mr. D. Jeyasingh, Senior Scale Lecturer in Economics, Pope's College, Mr. J. Jeyasingh, Senior Scale Lecturer in Economics, Pope's College Mr. M.A. Mohamed Shamsudeen, P.G. Assistant in English, Muslim Hr. Sec. School, Abiramam, Dr. V. Gopalkrishan, Head Department of Commerce, Aditanar College, Tiruchendur, Mr. S. Narayanarajan, Senior Scale Lecturer in Business Administration, Aditanar College and Mr. J.J. Gurusingh, Sawyerpuram, for their kind encouragement and support for the completion of the present research report.

I am also thankful to Late Mr. P. Israel, Head, Department of Zoology, Pope's College, who talked to me frequently and encouraged me to pursue my research project.

Above all, I thank God, Almighty, for showering His blessings to finish the work without which this humble piece of work would not have been appeared in its present form.

I remember my family members who were always with me in all my sorrows and happiness and provided moral and material support. I take this opportunity to express my deep sense of gratitude to my beloved parents, in-laws and my elder brother Mr. A. Arul Devadoss, Senior Scale Lecturer in History, St. John's College. My dear wife Mrs. Gracelin Julia Selvakumar and daughter Baby S. Leticia Mary were two silent witness of my struggling moments to complete this work. They spread me in my moments of grief and inspired me to continue the work. How can I leave them in this note!

Last but not least, I am very much thankful to my friend Mr. S.M.A. Syed Mohamed Khaja, Partner, Jasmine Computers, Malapalayam, Tirunelveli and other staff members Mr. K.H. Md. Sheik Mohideen, Mr. M.A. Md. Younoos, Mr. M Kaleefa, Mr. S. Khaji, Mr. J.S. Saleem and Mr. D. Karuppasamy for having typed several drafts of the manuscript including present report in an impressive manner.

A. Selvakumar

1

Introduction and Design of the Study

Child labour is a universal phenomenon. Its prevalence is seen almost in all periods of time. Until recently, few attempts have been made to understand its genesis and process, However, it is the declaration of the year 1979 as the International Year of the Child by the United Nations which has exposed the magnitude of the problem in its varied dimensions. The problem of child labour is rooted in the socio-economic conditions prevailing in a country. Children work under unsuitable conditions deterimental to their health and development. Childhood is the vital period of human life. Employment of children at an early age hampers their mental, physical and psychological growth. And this in turn affects severely the socio-economic and cultural growth of the country. However, child labour as a social problem has become and important component of welfare consciousness among the public, social organisations and the State. The problem of child labour is mankind's belated recognition that children are important, and that care for each stage of a child's growth is imperative if a nation is to prosper. In the present study, an attempt has been made to find out the socio-economic factors which play a significant role in pushing children into the labour force and the repercussions of early employment.

Every country wants its children to grow into good citizens. This can be achieved only through unrestricted but thoughtful and proper provision of all basic needs of life, i.e., good shelter, clothing, training and primary health care. Any inadequacy in them results in jeopardizing the lives of youngsters. They also need security, love, empathy and kind treatment.

HISTORICAL PERSPECTIVE

Since historical times, Child labour has existed in one form or another in all the societies of the world. Children of a primitive man, who used to lead the life of a food gatherer or hunter, helped him in his occupation. When a man started cultivation, children used to help him in comparatively lighter jobs. The joint family system, which was the main social institution at that time, provided the children with an atmosphere of security, warmth and compassion. With the passage of time, school-based education began, but it remained accessible largely to the privileged classes of the society.

The great Indian epics, *The Ramayana* and *The Mahabharata,* reveal that even the princes had to spend their childhood in, what might be termed as, training themselves to work. Rama, the hero of *Ramayana,* spent his childhood along with his younger brother Lakshman in the hermitage of sage Vashishta. The 'ashram' (hermitage) was a learning place where the two brothers not only mastered the marital arts but also helped their Guru (teacher) in his household chores and economic pursuits, e.g., collection of fruits and other eatables.[1]

In the other epic, Krishna, the hero of *Mahabharata,* spent his early childhood in the household of a chieftain of cowherds where he started grazing the cattle at a very young age of six years.[2]

Kutilya, the historian has referred to pleding of minors as slaves in his book *Arthasasthtra.* He recommended various kinds of punishments for selling or pledging a minor Arya individual. However, he felt that it was not an offence for foreigners and tribals to sell of pledge an offspring.[3]

In the medieval times, children were normally often employed as trainees under artisans and craftsmen. Certain crafts depended totally on the employment of children. The tradition still continues in carpet weaving or cotton and silk weaving industries. Even today, in India, these vocations employ a large number of children.

Furthermore, in a agrarian society, children work according to their capacities, and their work is always considered a part in the process of socialisation. Children of agriculturists have to perform specific tasks. Thus, many children are entrusted with the work that is time-consuming, while elders are busy with intensive, laborious and skilled tasks.[4]

The children of farmers' families start learning and functioning as participants and productive members of the family and community. Thus, children form an integral part of their agricultural household economy. They receive training for various work-roles and gradually start making a substantial contribution to their family income. In India, which is predominantly an agricultural country, a large number of children work in this sector even today.[5]

In pre-industrial Europe, boys helped their fathers in farms, herding cattle or scaring the birds form the crops. Girls would be set to spinning or looking after the babies.[6] In the 19th century Europe, for a number of jobs children were thought to be more suitable because of their small hands and slender/supple bodies. For instance, children were given the work of chimney sweeps.[7]

The technological revolution has increased the pace of industrialisation and urbanisation and has resulted in a significant change in the social scenario. The joint families, which were capable of providing a better sense of social and economic security to its members than such securities provided by nuclear families, started disintegrating. To survive, everyone in the family had to struggle hard. The new economic forces, unleashed by capitalism, destroyed the family based economy. A large number of labourers were displaced due to mechanisation of agriculture. The farmers were alienated from the land and driven from their homes in pursuit of work. They became wage-earning labourers. Extreme poverty created a situation in which the child had to be introduced to the labour market. Lack of alternative employment for adults and lack of education for children reinforced this process. The child's ability to grow and develop into a mentally and physically sound adult was severely restricted.[8]

Christopher Daniel says that in England, poor children as young as four, five or six years of age were set to work by being sold to farmers, by indenture to craftsmen or by hard labour in almshouses. These almshouses had utilised the cheap labour of children who had to work for more hours for lesser wages. Furthermore, Daniel observes: "Many died in their teens when they had to work themselves to death".[9] The arrogant entrepreneurs, with the intention of making more money, employed 'slappers' who held the young working children awake by whipping them when they fell asleep while working.[10]

Towards the middle of the 19th century, in the west the social ideology which was earlier in favour of child labour, started changing. Humanitarian argument started gaining support on the basis of dramatic cases of exhaustion, brutality and accidents in factories leading to deformities. In the case chimney sweeping, children were prone to accidents. Factory reforms were introduced to protect the children by fixing the minimum age of entry into work force, extending provisions concerning schooling provided by factory owner, barring employment at night or in underground mines or factories and working with dangerous material. Gradually, technological change and educational requirements tipped the balance of profitability away from child labour in factories and mills atleast, while restrictions on their labour made it harder to integrate their work with adult labour.[11]

The child labour that prevailed in the United States of America, was taken seriously and debated in the Children's

Bureau Conference on Child Welfare Standards in 1919.[12] The Industrial Revolution in Great Britain made child labour very common and widespread that it began spreading like a contagious disease in the European countries also in the course of time. There is a notion among people from various societies that "it was not for the family to support the child, rather it was for the child to support the family".[13]

In all primitive communities, children used to work according to their capacities. It was then considered a "Process of socialisation". To-day's children, however, are not necessarily working for the purpose of socialisation. They are assigned the specific goal of increasing their family income by their own earning.

In the case of children, the concept of the dignity of work, health care and training have specific meanings and scope. But, often such meanings are twisted to acquire short term benefits and thus children remain oppressed. Many children have to work for earning and not necessarily for learning. Unless it is the type of work that children willingly choose and that which serves the purpose of training with least damage to their overall development, employing children in labour force is a very unkind attitude on the part of adults. If children are willingly participating in a certain job, then that work could be considered a welcome labour as it brings them dignity of labour, even when the work remains remunerative. Moreover, this attitude cannot be harmful to any working child as it prevents the employer from exploiting the child.

Children are forced by socio-economic compulsions to work for their survival. They work either without wages at home or for a paltry income outside. They are denied their legitimate right to education, freedom and recreation. Thus, they turn out to be physically weak and mentally unsound, ultimately affecting the development of the society to which they belong.

Any child is an asset to his/her parents or the society or the nation. He or she would become an adult in years to come. This adult is expected to play an effective role in nation-building. Every child has to discharge the duties of a good citizen. But, this depends on the manner in which the child is allowed to grow into youth and subsequently adulthood. Concern about the child by various international bodies has resulted in the well thought-out United Nations Charter of Rights of Children and in the conventions and recommendations set forth by the International Labour Organisation.

MEANING AND DEFINITION

The term 'child labour' is used in a pejorative sense. It suggests something which is fateful and exploitative. Thus, child labour in a restricted sense means the employment of children in gainful occupations which are dangerous to their health and deny them the opportunities of development.

The term 'child labour' not only applies to the children working n industries but also to the children working in all forms of non-industrial occupations which are injurious to their physical, mental moral and social development.[14]

'Child Labour' refers to any work including domestic work performed by a persons usually below 14 years of age. Here child labour has been classified in low income countries into four categories. They are: Domestic work, Non-domestic and Non-monetary work, Bonded labour and Wage labour.[15]

V.V. Giri has distinguished the term 'child labour' in two sense, viz., an economic practice and a social evil. The first signifies the employment of children in gainful occupation with a view to adding to the income of the family, and the second, a broad aspect which takes into account the dangers to which the children are exposed which means the denial of opportunities of development.[16]

It is clear then that there are three essential aspects/ features which help one in detecting and identifying child labour. First, the child should be employed in gainful occupation; second the work to which he or she is exposed, must be dangerous to his or her health. Third, it must deny him or her the opportunity of development. Hence, any work extracted by a father from his child by making him work in his field or business place of long hours, is also covered under this definition, but work by students at school workshops cannot be called 'Child Labour'.[17]

The Encyclopaedia of Social Sciences defines child labour to be "... the business of wage earning or of participation in self or family support which conflicts directly or indirectly with the business of growth and education, the result is child labour".[18]

The diversity of opinion among researchers in defining child labour is due to differences in perceiving it as a social phenomenon. The Director General of the International Labour Organisation states that, "the first problem is defining the phenomenon relating to the notions of 'child work' and labour".[19] The most suitable and common definition of child labour is that, "Child labour can be conceived to include children under the age of 14 years in work or employment with the aim of earning a livelihood for themselves or for their families."[20]

The Gurupadaswamy Committee Report on Child Labour, 1979 points out that child labour is distinguished from work experience. It has mostly negative attributes. Work when taken up as a means for the fulfillment of some other needs, becomes enslaving in character and deleterious in its impact. Labour in the case of the child is especially harmful because the energy that should have been expanded on the nurturing of latent powers is consumed for purposes of bare survival.[21]

The Federal Children's Bureau condemns child labour in the following manner:

> The employment of young persons is a social problem whenever and wherever it deprives them of the opportunity for normal development. If children go to

work too soon or work under unfavourable conditions, the result is harmful not only to the individual but also to society. The problem should be visualised as a changing one, which lessens as higher standards are adopted, regulations improved, and employment restricted, but which increases as new light it shed upon the effects of industrial work on growing boys and girls.[22]

According to Rajani Kanta Das, the term 'Child Labour' refers to an economic practice and attendant social evil. Child labour as an economic practices signifies employment in gainful occupations and a material contribution to the labour income of the family; only and age-line differentiates if from adult labour.[23]

Any physical labour undertaken by a child below 15 years of age either under compulsion or voluntarily in an organised or unorgainsed sector, qualifies it to be called child labour.[24] Kulshreshtha writes that children working in all forms of industrial or non-industrial occupations which are not healthy to their physical, mental, moral and social development is convered under the definition of 'child labour'.[25] The word 'Child Labour' has been defined by Hammer-Flocks, Chairman of the United States Child Labour Committee as "any work by children that interferes with their physical development, their opportunities for desirable minimum education or their needed recreation".[26] According to Singh, the term 'child labour' applies to the children working in all forms of non-industrial occupations which are detrimental to their physical, mental, moral and social development.[27] B.M. Otta defines Child labour as "any activity performed by a child in the productive process in a more or less regular or casual basis with or without any remuneration attached to it".[28]

After considering the demographic, social and economic implications of the child labour, Naidu attempts to define Child Labour as that act which deprives them of educational opportunities, minimizes their chances for vocational training, stunts their physical growth, hampers their intellectual development and forces them to remain as unskilled labourers with low wages all their life.[29]

Child labor may be considered synonymous with an 'employed child', but both have to be distinguished from a 'working child'. Work does not deprive a child of formal education or recreation or other facilities enjoyed by a 'working child' in his/her family of procreation.[30]

The terms 'working child' and 'child labour' are often used synonymously. However, the former is quite descriptive and less precise in its meaning than the latter. Working children are those who are under 14 years of age and who do some work and receive returns in cash or kind or save money by rendering services for which the family would have to pay otherwise, these children may or may not continue the work with their schooling.[31]

On the other hand, 'employed child' implies some contractual relationship between employer and child. It includes helpers, part-time or full-time workers particularly in family enterprises.[32] According to Operations Research Group (ORG), "A working child is that child who was enumerated during the survey as a child falling within the 5-15 age bracket and who is at remunerative work may be paid or unpaid and busy and hour of the day within or outside the family".[33] Child work is work that contributes to normal growth and development of a child-physically, mentally, emotionally and spiritually".[34]

But, the term 'Child Labour' means both the 'employed child' and the 'Working Child'. It signifies employment of children in gainful occupations with a view to adding to the household income. However, it must be noted that children do not always work for monetary gains. It is not unusual to find them as unpaid workers, particularly in household industries. They contribute substantially to family labour. Moreover, children spend much of their time in household maintenance activities.[35]

OPERATIONAL DEFINITION

After considering these definitions of child labour carefully, the researcher presents the operational definition of this phenomenon under study as follows:

> Child labour may be defined as any activity performed by children of 14 and below 14 years of age, relating to beedi making on regular basis with or without remuneration. They are basically home workers carrying out the work in their homes themselves.

Every child labourer is first a child with all needs like other children. Children need opportunities not only for physical growth, but also for mental and personality growth through all activities and experiences of childhood. Wherever the business of wage earning or participation in family vocation conflicts directly or indirectly with the normal growth and education of a child, it results in child labour. Therefore, Chld labour begins with children involving themselves in work and thereby making the children forego the fulfillment of their needs both for present and future lives.

The measurement of child work cannot be done merely from the conventional point of view wherein the economic activities are alone considered. There is always a danger of exclusion of various such activities which are exploitative but otherwise appear very normal and common.

The main objective of the International Year of the Child was to sensitise decision makers, as well as the general public to the special needs of the children, to persuade the governments to give greater priority to problems concerning children and to stimulate and intensify actions directed towards the well being of children.

Every child has a right to receive the very best that the country can give him in education and training. The character of the national policy for children is that the country should give the utmost affection and care. That alone ensures the future of the children and their health. In a National Seminar held in February, 1964 M.L. Chagla the then Education Minister of India stated "I think the improvement of our human resources deserves as much, if not more, attention than the development of our material resources. Children are the invaluable human resource on whose development depends, in a large measure, the future of the nation".

It is relevant here to mention that by the term "compound beedi industry" this thesis refers to the area wherever beedi making, or work relating to beedi making, is undertaken. The word industry, hence, is not used here in a narrowed sense of a specific factory but is taken to include the whole network of contractors and employers and the workers (children) in beedi making.

MAGNITUDE OF THE PROBLEM

Society as much as never approved child labour. It is only the circumstances that make the society accept child labour, even if it is considered a social evil. Also, temperamentally a child can never work as strenuously as any adult would. So these 'Little Adults' if not kept employed, remain under constant threat of unemployment and thereby risk losing the source for their basic needs. An ironically, being exposed to 'Adult Life' at an early age works against child labour itself. As many of them are working for long hours even during night, with least protection from polluted environment at the place of work, and under constant mental and physical strain, their growth becomes stunted and some of them become useless for any other job in their adulthood that what they out of necessity do during their childhood. The work makes them susceptible to exploitation. Those who are working for wages are the most vulnerable to exploitation. In a few cases, those working without wages are also equally exploited.

As stated above, the children in their tender age, if given very odd jobs such as carrying heavy loads, working in polluting chemical plants, under unhygienic conditions grow physically and mentally abnormal.

Night work, continuous standing, sitting or using a single set of muscles, indoor confinement in noisy factories, exposure to dust and heat, carrying heavy loads, lifting heavy weights, contract with industrial poisons and the like are harmful to children. Carrying heavy loads and working in cramped areas in small factories can cause deformity, particularly in bones. Starting work at an early age has also been found to stunt physical growth, height, weight and normal expansion of the chest. Physically, children are not suited to long hours of strenuous and monotonous work. Their bodies suffer the effect of fatigue and exertion much more quickly than those of adults. Lack of adequate sleep caused due to long hours of work or night work and heavy work, increases the rate of accidents as well as reduces the growth of children. Children especially in the manufacturing sector are more prone to accidents and occupational hazards than those engaged in other jobs.

Working children are unable to participate in leisure and recreational activities and, therefore, lose the psycho-social benefits essential to their growth. It has been observed that a child labourer soon develops a habit of smoking and drinking. Some of them also become drug addicts or spend time in gambling, smuggling or similar criminal activities. Due to poverty, large number of working children are suffer from malnutrition. This lowers their resistance and makes them vulnerable to diseases of various types. Whenever children work in family vocations, they do not receive remuneration for their work, though their parents are benefited monetarily. Children develop the habit of borrowing money initially from their own houses, and later this leads them to incur larger debts from other sources outside.

Their employment does not allow the children to use profitably the educational and vocational facilities otherwise available to non-working children. Such a situation restrains their mental development. The attention span of children is shorter, compared to that of an adult, and hence they get bored soon. This would rather reduce the quality of production. Some situations are even harmful for their lives in the sense that children are more prone to accidents. Children being playful, carefree and lacking maturity of judgment, are more subject to accidents. The fatigue increases their predisposition to accidents. In certain concerns, they work harder than the adult workers. They work for hours together almost all the days of the week. They are forced to work themselves in over-crowded, dim and claustrophobic sheds and factory premises.

The children give up their studies, games and other childhood activities because their parents compel them to work in order to support their family monetarily. They are put to work even at the age of 5 or 6 years. They extract more work from their children. It is indeed an injustice done to them. In recent years, the problem of child labour has attracted the public consciousness persistently. The discussion pertaining to this was initiated when the government of India announced its intention to introduce a fresh legislation to deal with the phenomenon of child labour in 1985. As a result, the Child Labour (Prohibition and Regulation) Act came into effect in 1986.

Prior to this Act of 1986, the Indian Constitution prescribed certain provisions, for children, which are as follows:

1. Article 23 confers a fundamental right against certain forms of exploitation. The provisions of the Indian Penal Code provide the punishment for such exploitations and Article 23 gives a constitutional sanction to punishment.

2. Article 24 insists that 'no child below the age of 14 shall be employed to work in any factory or mine or engaged in any other hazardous employments.

3. Article 39 affirms that the state shall in particular, direct its policy towards securing:

(a) That the health and strength of the workers, women and men, and the tender age of children are not abused and that citizens are not forced by economic necessity to enter avocation unsuited to their age or strength, and

(b) The children and youth are protected against exploitation and against moral and material abandonment.

4. Articles 42 and 43 provided for securing just and human conditions of work and hold out a promise that the state shall endeavour to secure by suitable legislation or economic organisation or in any other, to all workers agricultural, industrial or otherwise, a living wage, better conditions of work, ensuring a decent standard of life and full employment with leisure and social and cultural opportunities.[36]

The legislative enactments such as, the Factories Act, 1948 and the Minimum Wages Act, 1948 provide legal protection to children in various occupations, However, these Acts including the Child Labour (Prohibition and Regulation) Act, 1986 have not tackled the problem of child labour yet.

At the World Summit For Children held on 30 September 1990, it was agreed to put an end to the practice of child labour. The Summit also focused its attention on the welfare of the children pursuing legitimate employment. It further recommended various strategies to deal with the problem of child labour in general and healthy upbringing of children in particular.[37]

The Article 32 in Convention on the Rights of the Child adopted by the General Assembly of the United Nations on 20 November 1989 declares:

1. State Parties recognize the right of the child to be protected from economic explication and (also) from performing any work that is likely to be hazardous or to interfere with the child's education, or to be

harmful to the child's health or physical, mental, spiritual, moral or social development.

2. States Parties shall take legislative, administrative, social and educational measures to ensure the implementation of the present Article. To this end, and having regard to the relevant provisions of other international instruments, States Parties shall in particular:

   (a) Provide for a minimum age or minimum ages for admission to employment;

   (b) Provide for appropriate regulations of the hours and conditions of employment;

   (c) Provide for appropriate penalties or other sanctions to ensure the effective enforcement of the present Article.[38]

Child labour is an economic practice as well as a social problem. It is an economic practice as it involves the economically unsound parents to compel their children to work in certain jobs to earn money. The children contribute substantially to their family income. Thus, from the parents' point of view, compelling children to do available work in their home is an accepted practice.

India has the largest child labour force employed in mostly hazardous industries. The Child Labour (Prohibition and Regulation) Act, 1986 was enacted to ban child labour in industries and regulate its conditions. But, the main reason for the prevalence of this problem in India is the lack of proper enforcement of this Act.

The idea of child labour seems to have its base in ancient thinking. As an illustration of this, one may refer to the belief found in the developing countries; for many parents in working class families, majority of the children are extra earners increasing the family income. This belief is, whether justified or not, a tradition oriented one, handed down from generation to generation. In the view of Elias Mendelievich. "This idea stems not so much from poverty as from the traditional belief that there is a no point in making any plans beyond those for satisfying the family's immediate basic needs".[39] Therefore, majority of the parents do not care to better the prospects of their children. But, on the other hand, they are ready to exploit them. As a result, the children become an integral part of the household economy, which happens to be a curse of their life.

There is some element of truth in the statement of Mendelievich. It would be observed that children are getting a pleasant life from their earnings. So, they are compelled to go for a job at an early age. As long as they are not compelled to go to school, they are happy. Also, their parents do not bother about their future.

Child labour is equally a social problem in the sense that millions of children in the world are economically exploited by their families, while they seek security and love from their parents. This type of exploitation is a social injustice. Thus, child labour is a socio-economic phenomeonon.[40]

Parents force their children to work as early as possible instead of allowing them to go to school and enjoy a carefree childhood. Parents of poor families and low castes put their children to work. Gangrade observes: "For them, uneducated children are an asset, and the desire to educate them becomes a double liability because of, first, the loss of earning of the child who does not work, and second the expenditure involved in education, however low it may be".[41] Particularly in developing countries, children are employed at an early age instead of getting primary education. Also they have to take the responsibility to support their old, unemployed and unhealthy parents.

The condition of the girls children worse when compared with that of boys. They are involved in beediworks at the age of four or five in. They have to work very hard every day. The parents are encouraging their sons to study atleast upto primary or middle school level. But, they do not encourage their daughters to do so. According to them, getting vast experience and knowledge in beedi making is an essential qualification for their daughters to get married. Therefore, their daughters have to make some quantity of beedis every day. Otherwise they are punished. Suppose, on a particular day, the girls are not able to complete the prescribed quota, they have to borrow beedis from the professional beedi lenders with an interest. For instance, Dharamalingam in his study observes that a 12 year old girls in a village in Tirunelveli District was under tremendous pressure from her parents. So, she started borrowing beedis. Soon the girl was deeply in debt. Realising that she could not pay back, the lender informed her parents. Fearing that her mother would beat her, the girl committed suicide by consuming the seeds of a wild plant. This kind of discrimination against girls would lead them to such an end or cause psychological complications.[42]

The practice of employing children in hazardous work would affect their physical as well as mental health. They are made to work for hours together in a day. Normally, they work for 10-12 hours per day. In course of time, they would be subject to occupational diseases even during their childhood. Especially they are mostly susceptible to respiratory diseases such as chronic bronchitis and tuberculosis.

The child workers are employed in certain places where an adult worker refuses to work. Neera Burra observes that in certain occupations, workers are allowed to come into contact with harmful substances like chemicals as in case of balloons, glass, match and fireworks and lock industries. These industries emit fumes, dust or cotton fluff that damage lungs or any other organ of body. The children working in such industries are exposed to various health hazards.[43] Besides the nature of their occupation, malnutrition and under nutrition would double the health problems among the child workers.[44]

Child Labour is as serious problem confronting the world societies. Rodgers and Standing say that the greater the degree of drudgery of the work, the lesser the possibility of children acquiring knowledge and skill through their work. They also observe that the child's participation in labour force activities tends to reduce their potential for educational development. They point out that the work assigned to children weakens their resistance to illness and decrease their life expectancy. According to them, high levels of adult employment and widespread poverty push children into unskilled, unsafe and low-income labour market.[45]

A report on child labour suggests that the elimination of this problem would increase the employment opportunities for atleast fifteen million unemployed adults.[46] But it is important to note that it may lead a number of families to succumb to starvation as the major income earned by the child workers is stopped. Therefore, alternative measures for earning income should be given to those families by the Government.

Though child labour is prevalent all over the world, it is alarmingly widespread in South Asia where it is reported that about 29 million children are engaged as work force.[47] In post-industrialised India, the children were employed in cotton and jute mills and coal mines as wage workers. However, at present, several thousands of children are employed mostly in cottage industries such as beediworks, matchworks, fireworks, agarbatti manufacture, handloom weaving, leather tannery, glass bangles making, carpet weaving, mat weaving, carpentry, pottery, tailoring and the like. The major sector which employs a large section of children is agriculture. In urban areas, children are working as domestic servants, and they are found to work in hotels and restaurants, automobile tinkering and fueling stations, small workshops and repair-shops and brick-kilns or construction.

In industrialised countries, child labour still exists. In Southern Europe, there has always been relatively a large number of children working for a wage, particularly engaged in seasonal activities, street trades, small workshops or in a homework setting. Child labour also exists in the countries of Northern Europe, as was recently shown in a survey conducted in the United Kingdom. A substantial increase in child labour has also been observed in several Central and East European countries as a result of the difficulties faced by large sections of population due to the emergence of market economy. The same is true of the United States, where the growth of the service sector, the rapid increase in the supply of part-time jobs and the search for a more flexible work force have contributed to the expansion of the child labour market. Participation rates of children in economic activity are much higher in rural than in urban areas.

According to the estimates of Non-governmental Organisation, the number of child labourers could be between 44 and 100 million. According to an estimate of the International Labour Organisation (1996), there were 12.66 million full time and 10.50 million marginal child workers. Whatever may be the actual figure of child labour, the important point is that child labour phenomenon in India is on the rise and it shows that India has a substantial and increasing number of working children. Hence, the country needs to take various measures on warfooting to curb this evil.[49]

Various surveys reveal that the number of working children in the world is 200 millions.[50] In India, according to the 1991 Census, the total work force of children is 1, 12, 85, 349 in the age group of 0-14. Of these workers, 54.85 per cent are boys and 45.15 per cent are girls. Of the total number of child workers, 80.48 per cent are main workers and 19.52 per cent are marginal workers. Among the total child workers, 90.85 per cent are rural workers and 9.15 per cent are urban workers. Out of the total number of child workers, 48.36 per cent are rural boys and 42.50 per cent are rural girls. Child workers comprise 6.49 per cent of urban

Table 1.1: State-wise Distribution of Child Workers (0-14 Age Group) According to 1971, 1981 and 1991 Census

Sl. No.	State/Union Territories	Child Workers in the Age Group of 0-14				
		1971	1981	1991		
				Main Child Workers	Marginal Child Workers	Total no. of Child Workers
1.	Andhra Pradesh	1,627,492	1,951,312	1,537,293	124,647	1,661,940
2.	Assam	239,349*	**	259,953	67,645	327,598
3.	Bihar	1,059,359	1,101,764	795,444	146,801	942,245
4.	Gujarat	518,061	616,913	373,027	150,558	523,585
5.	Haryana	137,826	194,189	89,030	20,661	109,691
6.	Himachal Pradesh	71,384	99,624	30,771	25,667	56,438
7.	Jammu and Kashmir	70,489	258,437	0	0	0
8.	Karnataka	808,719	1,131,530	818,159	158,088	976,247
9.	Kerala	111,801	92,854	28,590	6,210	34,800
10.	Madhya Pradesh	1,112,319	1,698,597	997,940	345,623	1,352,583
11.	Maharashtra	988,357	1,557,756	805,847	262,571	1,068,418
12.	Manipur	16,380	20,217	13,478	3,015	16,493
13.	Meghalaya	30,440	44,916	30,730	3,903	34,633
14.	Nagaland	13,726	16,235	16,106	378	16,476
15.	Orissa	492,477	702,293	325,250	127,144	452,394
16.	Punjab	232,774	216,939	132,144	10,454	142,868

(Contd...)

17.	Rajasthan	587,389	819,605	490,522	283,677	774,199
18.	Sikkim	15,661	8,561	5,254	344	5,598
19.	Tamil Nadu	713,305	957,055	523,125	55,764	578,889
20.	Tripura	17,490	24,204	13,506	2,972	16,478
21.	Uttar Pradesh	1,326,726	1,434,675	1,145,087	264,999	1,410,086
22.	West Bengal	511,443	605,263	593,387	118,304	711,691
23.	Andaman & Nikobar Island	572	1,309	758	507	1,265
24.	Arunachal Pradesh	17,925	17,950	11,632	763	12,395
25.	Chandigarh	1,086	1,986	1,839	31	1,870
26.	Dadra & Nagar Haveli	3,102	3,615	2,677	1,739	4,416
27.	Delhi	17,120	25,717	26,670	681	27,351
28.	Daman and Diu	7,391	9,378	741	200	941
29.	Goa	0	0	3,938	718	4,656
30.	Lakshadweep	97	56	17	17	34
31.	Mizoram	***	6,314	6,391	10,020	16,411
32.	Pondicherry	3,725	3,606	2,565	115	2,660
	Total	10,753,985	13,640,870	9,082,141	2,203,208	11,285,349

* Includes figures of Mizo district also which then formed part of Assam.

** 1981 Census could not be conducted in Assam due to disturbed conditions prevailing there then.

*** Census figures of 1971 in respect of Mizoram included under Assam.

Source: Census Report, 1991. Government of India.

Table 1.2: State-wise Distribution of Main Child Workers According to 1991 Census

Sl. No.	State/Union Territories	Main Child Workers						
		Rural			Urban			
		Male	Female	Total no. of Workers	Male	Female	Total no. of Workers	Total no. of Child Workers
1.	Andhra Pradesh	689,053	716,469	1,405,522	87,835	43,936	131,771	1,537,293
2.	Assam	182,946	61,382	244,328	8,219	7,406	15,625	259,953
3.	Bihar	550,281	201,125	751,406	36,560	7,478	44,038	95,444
4.	Gujarat	203,672	119,307	322,979	41,448	8,600	50,048	373,027
5.	Haryana	60,050	18,003	78,053	9,346	1,631	10,977	89,030
6.	Himachal Pradesh	13,113	16,688	29,801	642	328	970	30,7771
7.	Jammu and Kashmir			0		0	0	0
8.	Karnataka	387,464	321,543	709,007	73,978	35,174	109,152	818,159
9.	Kerala	12,560	9,430	21,990	3,692	2,908	6,600	28,590
10.	Madhya Pradesh	534,732	405,354	940,086	40,903	16,951	57,854	997,940
11.	Maharashtra	329,540	381,068	710,608	69,005	26,234	95,239	805,847
12.	Manipur	5,438	6,968	12,406	504	568	1,072	13,478
13.	Meghalaya	17,415	12,220	29,635	536	559	1,095	30,730
14.	Nagaland	7,134	8,308	15,442	434	230	664	16,106
15.	Orissa	206,052	101,882	307,934	12,389	4,927	17,316	325,250
16.	Punjab	102,636	8,178	110,814	19,502	2,098	21,600	132,414

(Contd...)

17. Rajasthan	247,817	205,011	452,828	28,502	9,192	37,694	490,522
18. Sikkim	2,373	2,511	4,884	211	159	370	5,254
19. Tamil Nadu	208,875	215,865	424,740	61,974	36,411	98,385	523,125
20. Tripura	8,246	4,224	12,470	487	549	1,066	13,506
21. Uttar Pradesh	782,682	210,672	993,353	1,33,068	18,665	151,733	1,145,087
22. West Bengal	395,695	127,881	523,576	47,012	22,799	69,811	593,387
23. Andaman & Nikobar Island	438	141	579	151	28	179	758
24. Arunachal Pradesh	4,734	6,285	11,019	344	269	613	11,632
25. Chandigarh	243	34	277	1,265	295	1,562	1,839
26. Dadra & Nagar Haveli	1,2058	1,379	2,584	50	43	93	2,677
27. Delhi	1,758	380	2,138	21,616	2,916	24,532	26,670
28. Daman and Diu	355	271	626	75	40	115	741
29. Goa	909	1,092	2,001	1,220	717	1,937	3,938
30. Lakshadweep	3	1	4	13	0	13	17
31. Mizoram	2,415	2,717	5,132	672	587	1,259	6,391
32. Pondicherry	557	426	983	1,182	400	1,582	2,565
Total	4,960,391	3,166,815	8,127,206	702,835	252,100	954,935	9,082,141

Source: Census Report, 1991. Government of India.

Table 1.3: State-wise Distribution of Main Child Workers According to 1991 Census

Sl. No.	State/Union Territories	Marginal Child Workers						
		Rural			Urban			
		Male	*Female*	*Total no. of Workers*	*Male*	*Female*	*Total no. of Workers*	*Total no. of Child Workers*
1.	Andhra Pradesh	27,761	91,616	119,377	1,853	3,417	5,270	124,647
2.	Assam	16,395	50,750	67,145	190	310	500	67,645
3.	Bihar	31,314	112,512	143,826	923	2,052	2,975	146,801
4.	Gujarat	16,199	128,939	145,138	1,688	3,732	5,420	150,558
5.	Haryana	3,961	16,320	20,281	190	190	380	20,661
6.	Himachal Pradesh	8,771	16,592	25,363	151	153	304	25,667
7.	Jammu and Kashmir			0			0	0
8.	Karnataka	35,319	117,867	153,206	1,880	3,002	4,882	158,088
9.	Kerala	2,670	2,630	5,300	440	470	910	6,210
10.	Madhya Pradesh	84,987	260,579	345,566	3,070	5,987	9,057	354,623
11.	Maharashtra	67,256	184,698	251,954	5,341	5,276	10,617	262,571
12.	Manipur	861	1,495	2,356	180	479	659	3,015
13.	Meghalaya	1,434	2,401	3,835	27	41	68	3,903
14.	Nagaland	185	178	363	3	4	7	370
15.	Orissa	26,122	99,225	125,347	660	1,137	1,797	127,144
16.	Punjab	1,560	8,506	10,066	208	180	388	10,454

(Contd...)

17. Rajasthan	51,363	26,654	278,017	1,349	4,311	5,660	283,677
18. Sikkim	124	188	312	22	10	32	344
19. Tamil Nadu	7,323	44,670	51,993	1,012	2,759	3,771	55,764
20. Tripura	833	2,100	2,933	10	29	39	2,972
21. Uttar Pradesh	66,367	184,270	250,637	5,465	8,897	14,362	264,999
22. West Bengal	41,858	71,585	113,423	2,675	2,206	4,881	118,304
23. Andaman & Nikobar Island	253	247	500	7	0	7	507
24. Arunachal Pradesh	192	568	760	3	0	3	763
25. Chandigarh	6	8	14	12	5	17	31
26. Dadra & Nagar Haveli	535	1,193	1,728	2	9	11	1,739
27. Delhi	61	55	116	341	224	565	681
28. Daman and Diu	31	111	142	21	37	58	200
29. Goa	207	407	614	43	61	104	718
30. Lakshadweep	8	1	9	4	4	8	17
31. Mizoram	2,685	2,927	5,612	2,153	2,255	4,408	10,020
32. Pondicherry	19	42	61	25	29	54	115
Total	496,660	1,629,334	2,125,994	29,948	47,266	77,214	2,203,208

Source: Census Report, 1991. Government of India.

Table 1.4: Child Labour in some Sectors in India

Sl. No.	Industry	Location	Total no. of Workers	Child Workers	Percentage of Child Workers in Total No. of Workers
1.	Slate Pencil	Mandsaur, Madhya Pradesh	12,000	1,000	8.30
2.	Slate	Markapur, Andhra Pradesh	15,000	3,750 (app.)	25.00
3.	Diamond Cutting	Surat, Gujarat	1,00,000	15,000	15.00
4.	Agata Cutting	Cambay, Gujarat	30,000	Not known	
5.	Gem Polishing	Jaipur, Rajasthan	60,000	13,600	22.60
6.	Power loom	Bhiwanti, Maharashtra	3,00,000	15,000	5.00
7.	Cotton hosiery	Tiruppur, Tamil Nadu	30,000	8,000	33.33
8.	Carpet Weaving	Mirzapur-Bhadohi, Uttar Pradesh	2,00,000	1,50,000	75.00
9.	Carpet Weaving	Jammu & Kashmir	4,00,000 app.	1,00,000	25.00
10.	Carpet Weaving	Rajasthan	30,000	12,000	40.00
11.	Lock-making	Aligarh, Uttar Pradesh	80,000	7,000	8.70

(Contd...)

12.	Pottery	Khurja, Uttar Pradesh	20,000	5,000	25.00
13.	Brass Ware	Moradabad, Uttar Pradesh	1,50,000	40,000	26.60
14.	Match	Sivakasi, Tamil Nadu	Not known	45,000	-
15.	Glass	Firozabad, Uttar Pradesh	2,00,000	50,000	25.00
16.	Silk & Products	Varanasi, Uttar Pradesh	3,512	1,108	31.50
17.	Knives	Rampur, Uttar Pradesh	Not known	3,000	-
18.	Handicrafts	Jammu & Kashmir	90,000	26,178	29.42
19.	Silk Weaving	Bihar	Not known	10,000	-
20.	Brocade & Zari Industry	Varanasi and other Centres, Uttar Pradesh	Not known	3,00,000	-
21.	Brick-Kilns	West Bengal	Not known	35,000	-
22.	Beedi	India	32,75,000	3,27,500	10.00
23.	Circus Industry	40 Major Circuses	-	12% of the Labour Strength	-
24.	Handloom and Handi Crafts	Jammu & Kashmir	1,16,000	28,348	25.00

Source: Neera Burra, *Born to work* (Delhi: Oxford University Press,), pp. xxii-xxiv.

boys and 2.65 per cent of urban girls (Refer to tables 1.1, 1.2 & 1.3 in the present chapter of this research report).

In Tamil Nadu, the total work force of children is 5,78,889. Of these child workers, 48.22 per cent are boys and 51.78 per cent are girls. Of the child workers, 90.37 per cent are main workers and 9.63 per cent are marginal workers. Among the total work force of children, 82.35 per cent are rural workers and 17.65 per cent are urban workers. Out of the total number of child workers, 37.35 per cent are rural boys and 45 per cent are rural girls. Total number of child workers comprise of 10.88 per cent of urban boys and 6.77 per cent of urban girls (Refer to tables 1.1, 1.2 & 1.3 of this chapter).

The census data reveal that during 1961-71, the number of child workers in India declined from 14.5 million to 10.8 million. During 1981, the number has gone up again. But, during 1991, it has again declined. These ups and downs express a more definitive, conceptual and statistical problem than any change in the incidence of child labour as such.

The status of child labour seems to vary considerably among the major States in India. Andhra Pradesh has the largest population of child labour, Nagaland has the lowest. It is also a fact that there are more boys than girls among the child workers.

In Tamil Nadu, concentration of child labour is high in the districts of Vellore, Erode, Coimbatore, Ramanathapuram, Trichy, Madurai, Virudhunagar, Tuticorin and Tirunelveli. This shows that the problem of child labour is more serious in these districts than in the other districts.

In Tamil Nadu, 32 per cent of the total number of child workers are non-agricultural workers. They are working at fireworks at Sivakasi in Virudhunagar District and the beediworks in Tirunelveli, Tiruchirapalli and Vellore districts.[51] Beedi is a common locally made cigarette.

In all the districts of Tamil Nadu, working girls are more than the working boys according to the 1991 census.

This shows that more girls than boys are subject to several problems caused by child labour. It is estimated that in Tirunelveli district, there are about 2,00,000 child labourers employed in various jobs. Of them, girls outnumber the boys.

In spite of the fact that more child labourers are employed in several unorganised sectors, the children engaged in beedi making are selected for the present study because of the following reasons:

(i) It is, unlike other industries, not subject to competition from modern industries;

(ii) It does not need any protective treatment as beedis can be easily shifted from house to house and village to village;

(iii) It is classified as an unorganised sector falling under the small scale and cottage industries;

(iv) It attracts many traditional occupationists.

Beedi companies in India employ more than 2.5 million workers; of them about 90 per cent of workers are women and children.[52] They are working in their homes with the raw material brought from local contractors. They work on the basis of piece-rate wage. Most rural people earn their income mainly from beedi making. A large number of children join their parents in their work. They work for 10-12 hours per day. Thus, the child labour in beediworks has an urgent need for analysis.

However, there are only few studies that examine how this industry is carried on, how it contributes to an increased household income, and how it affects health and social status of the workers concerned. The limited coverage in this area has made the researcher study these other aspects of the beediworks, focusing mainly on child labour.

In India, 32,75,000 beedi workers are engaged in this work. Out of the total number of workers, 10 per cent of them are child workers in the beediworks (Refer to table 1.4 of this chapter).

Beedi manufacturing has been an important activity in about 2,000 centres in Tamil Nadu for the past eighty years. The state ranks fifth among the beedi manufacturing states in India, with the first four states being Maharashtra, Madhya Pradesh, Kerala and West Bengal. The industry was strongly localised even in the first decade of the present century in Chennai, Vellore (neighbouring areas in Vellore District) and the Mukkudal area in Tirunelveli district.[53]

In Tamil Nadu, Tirunelveli and Vellore districts are important centers for beedi manufacturing. There are about 300 big beedi companies and 3,000 to 4,000 contractors with about 10,00,000 workers in these companies.[54] Of them, Tirunelveli district consists of over 40 per cent of the beedi manufacturing units, and nearly one-third of the contractors and sub-contractors.

In Tamil Nadu, next to agriculture, beedi making is a major occupation. Children are engaged in beedi making. The total number of girl child workers is higher than that of boy child workers. As a result, 63,000 child labourers are engaged in beedi making according to a recent survey conducted by the District Collectorate.

In Tirunelveli district beedi making is widely prevalent in various blocks, viz., Palayamkottai, Pappakudi, Keelapavoor, Alangulam, Kadayam, Tenkasi, Sankarankoil and Radhapuram. There are sixty leading manufacturers in the district. In the district, child labourers engaged in beedi making are more concentrated in certain areas, viz., Melapalayam (Palayamkottai block), Mukkudal (Pappakudi block), Keelapavoor, Kadayam, Alangulam and Tenkasi.

METHODOLOGY

The main focus of the present study is on the nature of work, age, income, educational standard, health, working conditions, legal intervention and exploitation of child workers. These aspects are, in one way or another, related to the policies concerning child labour. Though there are studies on the causes of child labour and its socio-economic aspects, only a few have dealt with child labour in the beedi industry. Therefore, the present study intends to fill this gap.

STATEMENT OF THE PROBLEM

In pursuance of the objectives framed, Tirunelveli District has been selected since beedi manufacturing is a more common in this district than in any other district of Southern Tamil Nadu. This district produces beedis on a large scale by employing several thousands of children with other female adult workers. In the Tamil Nadu beedi industry, Tirunelveli District is second only to the Vellore District in extracting child labour. In 1995, the Tirunelveli District Administration organised a quick survey with the assistance of a group of government employees and volunteers to find out the total number of child labourers in the beediworks and other sectors in this district. The survey reports that altogether there are 63,376 children (5-15 years) employed in various jobs. They comprise of 23,898 boys (37.74 per cent) and 39,418 girls (62.26 per cent). Of them, 23,488 children (37.10 per cent) are beedi workers comprising of 1,311 boys (5.58 per cent) and 22,177 girls (94.42 per cent). The rest of them (39,828 or 62,90 per cent) are engaged in other jobs; and of which 22,587 (56.71 per cent) are boys and 17,241 (43.29 per cent) are girls. The sex-wise and area-wise distribution of child workers is given in Table1.5.

The table, makes it clear that a majority of girls are engaged in the beediworks whereas a majority of boys are engaged in other works. In beedi industry, a large majority of girl children are working. The ratio of boys and girls engaged in this work, is about 1:10. Likewise, the proportion of female beedi workers is more than thrice the proportion of male beedi workers. Thus, it is clear that more female workers than the male workers are engaged in beedimaking. Therefore, it is concluded that, beedi industry has a large number of girl child workers and women workers.

Table 1.5: Proportion of Working Children (5-15 Years) in the District by Area and Sex

Sl. No.	*Area*	*Beediworks*			*Other works*		
		Boys	*Girls*	*Total*	*Boys*	*Girls*	*Total*
	Municipality						
1.	Tirunelveli	1.39	61.33	36.95	98.61	38.67	63.05
2.	Palayamkottai	0.43	35.93	20.19	99.57	64.07	79.81
3.	Melapalayam	33.45	89.16	71.50	66.55	10.84	28.50
4.	Sankarankoil	0.20	7.68	4.63	99.80	92.32	95.37
5.	Tenkasi	6.13	57.42	37.08	93.87	42.58	62.92
6.	Kadayanallur	2.58	45.71	27.08	97.42	54.29	62.92
7.	Shenkottai	0.67	84.05	53.45	99.33	15.95	46.55
8.	Puliyankudi	24.19	66.90	49.59	75.81	33.10	50.41
	Blocks						
1.	Palayamkottai	1.46	40.66	28.58	98.54	59.54	71.42
2.	Manur	1.23	74.89	47.42	98.77	25.11	52.58
3.	Melaneelithanallur	-	7.92	4.28	100.00	92.08	95.72
4.	Sankarankoil	9.25	24.46	17.54	90.75	75.54	82.46

(Contd...)

5.	Cheranmahadevi	0.27	64.48	43.14	99.73	35.52	56.86
6.	Pappakudi	28.76	56.34	44.36	71.24	43.66	55.64
7.	Ambasamudram	-	74.39	44.82	100.00	25.61	55.18
8.	Kadayam	3.44	76.91	47.36	96.56	23.09	52.64
9.	Nanguneri	-	62.73	33.83	100.00	37.27	66.17
10.	Kalakkadu	22.81	73.63	48.90	77.19	26.37	51.10
11.	Valliyur	-	56.89	42.06	100.00	43.11	57.94
12.	Radhapuram	1.57	45.12	24.35	98.43	54.88	75.65
13.	Alangulam	24.39	89.78	78.53	75.61	10.22	21.47
14.	Keelapavoor	5.12	93.28	62.76	94.88	6.72	37.24
15.	Tenkasi	-	71.66	49.59	100.00	28.34	50.41
16.	Shenkottai	0.11	75.96	51.48	99.89	24.04	48.52
17.	Kadayanallur	0.57	67.54	40.45	99.43	32.46	59.55
18.	Vasudevanallur	1.66	41.18	26.69	98.34	58.82	73.31
19.	All together	5.49	56.26	37.10	94.51	43.74	62.90

Source: District Collectorate, Tirunelveli.

OBJECTIVES OF THE STUDY

The study has been carried out with the objectives to assess and examine the following:

1. Whether the income of the family is increased considerably due to the employment of children;
2. The levels of exploitation of child labourers;
3. The impact of legal intervention on child labour;
4. The lealth problems of child labourers.

SAMPLE DESIGN

Multi-stage sampling method has been used in the present study. The selection of samples involved different stages. A list of all areas in Tirunelveli District, where beedi making is the main occupation for a considerable section of population was prepared. They are various blocks such as, Keelapavoor, Pappakudi, Kadayam, Alangulam, Tenkasi, Shenkottai, Sankarankoil, Radhapuram, Kalakkadu, Ambasamudram and Melapalayam town. Of them, the first five blocks and the Melapalayam town were selected as sample areas on the basis of judgment sampling method because they consist of a large number of beedi workers, both adults and children. The Melapalayam town, 24 villages in Keelapavoor block, 18 villages in Pappakudi block, 16 villages in Kadayam block, 13 villages in Alangulam block, 8 villages and a town in Tenkasi block areas were selected on the basis of random sampling method. This gives a total of 81 sample areas. Of them, the families engaged in beediworks were enumerated. From the total number of these families, the households consisting of child labour upto 14 years were identified. After enumerating the child labourers from those households, 500 children were selected as samples on the basis of random sampling method. Accordingly, a sample of 500 households were drawn from Melapalayam (125), Keelapavoor block (100), Pappakudi block (85), Kadayam block (75), Alangulam block (65) and Tenkasi block (50). It was done so in order to facilitate a comparison between rural and urban child labourers.

The survey covered two types of informants, viz., the child workers and their parents. It is imperative a comprehensive study on child labour should focus necessarily on the two categories of respondents. And conclusions were drawn from the analysis of data collected from these respondents.

SAMPLING FRAME

Stage 1	:	Selection of areas where beedi making is the main occupation for a considerable section of population in the district on the basis of judgment sampling method.
Stage 2	:	Selection of areas consisting of a large number number of children in beediworks on the basis of judgment sampling method.
Stage 3	:	Selection of representative areas from the regions already selected on the basis of judgment sampling method. (altogether 81 areas selected)
Stage 4	:	Enumeration of families in which children are involved in beediworks in all the 81 areas selected.
Stage 5	:	Selection of 500 households from the total households enumerated, on the basis of random sampling method.
Stage 6	:	Survey of child labourers and their households.

TOOLS OF DATA COLLECTION

I. Interview-schedule

The present study is an empirical one. Survey method was employed to collect the data from the child labourers and their parents. So, an interview-schedule was prepared and applied. The data used for the present study were primary in nature. And an interview-schedule was prepared since the respondents, by and large, belonged to the low educational category and were found to be totally incapable of answering

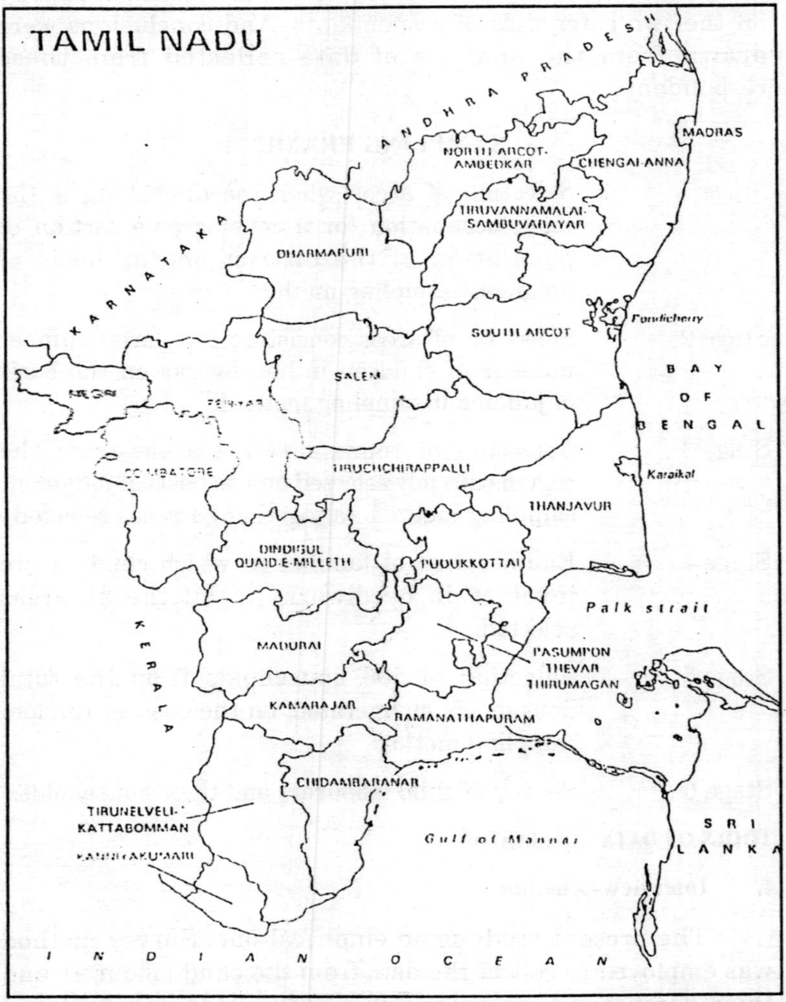
TAMIL NADU
ANDHRA PRADESH
KARNATAKA
MADRAS
NORTH ARCOT-AMBEDKAR
CHENGAI-ANNA
TIRUVANNAMALAI-SAMBUVARAYAR
DHARMAPURI
SOUTH ARCOT
Pondicherry
BAY OF BENGAL
SALEM
COIMBATORE
TIRUCHCHIRAPPALLI
Karaikal
THANJAVUR
DINDIGUL QUAID-E-MILLETH
PUDUKKOTTAI
Palk strait
KERALA
MADURAI
PASUMPON THEVAR THIRUMAGAN
KAMARAJAR
RAMANATHAPURAM
CHIDAMBARANAR
TIRUNELVELI-KATTABOMMAN
Gulf of Mannar
SRI LANKA
INDIAN OCEAN

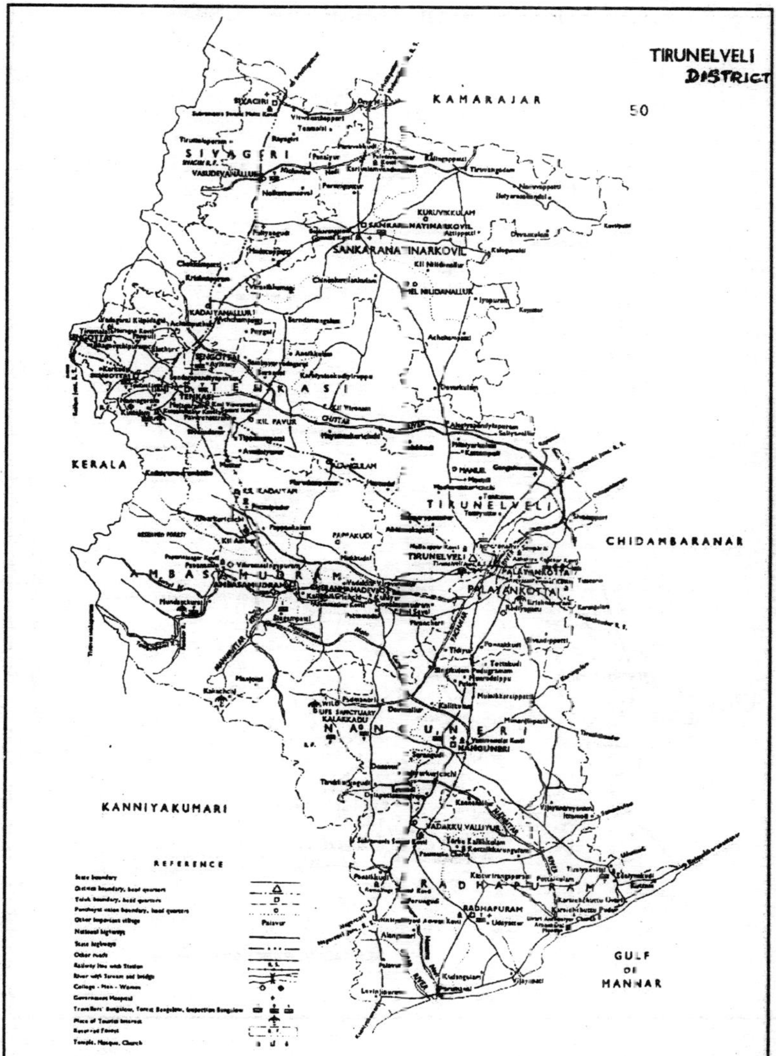
TIRUNELVELI
DISTRICT
KAMARAJAR
SIVAGIRI
SANKARANAINARKOVIL
TENKASI
KERALA
TIRUNELVELI
CHIDAMBARANAR
AMBASAMUDRAM
PALAYANKOTTAI
NANGUNERI
KANNIYAKUMARI
RADHAPURAM
GULF
OF
MANNAR
REFERENCE

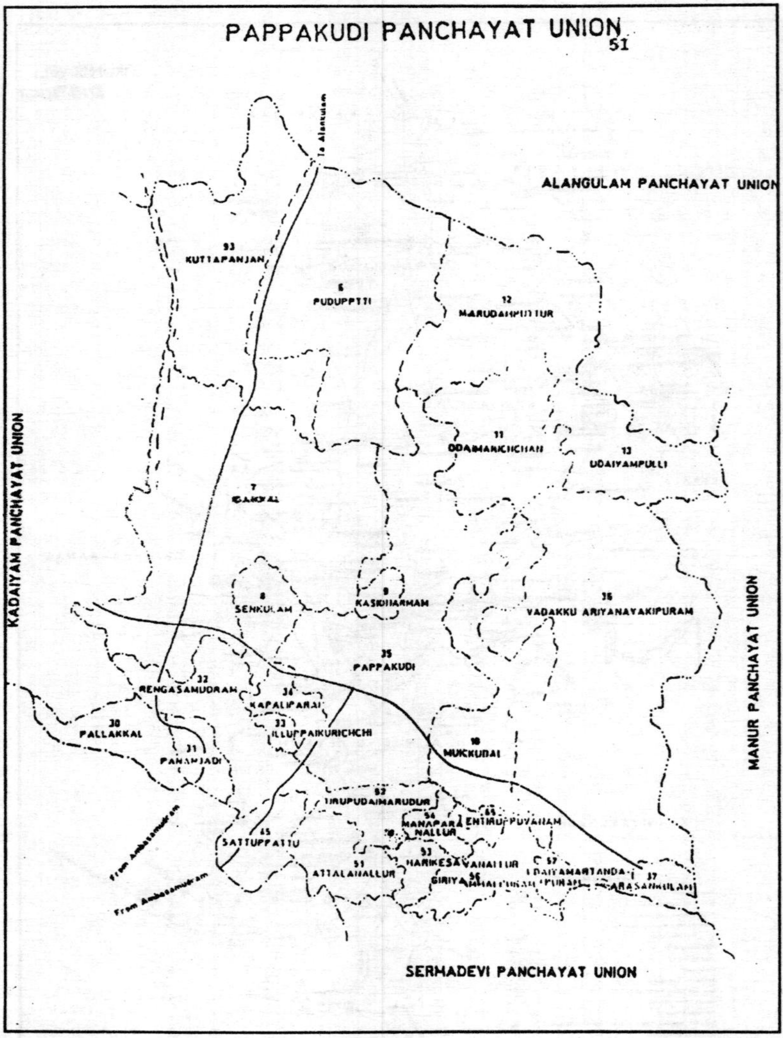
PAPPAKUDI PANCHAYAT UNION
ALANGULAM PANCHAYAT UNION
KADAIYAM PANCHAYAT UNION
MANUR PANCHAYAT UNION
SERMADEVI PANCHAYAT UNION
KUTTAPANJAN
PUDUPPTTI
MARUDAMPUTTUR
UDAIYAMPULLI
SENKULAM
PAPPAKUDI
VADAKKU ARIYANAYAKIPURAM
RENGASAMUDRAM
KAPALIPARAI
PALLAKKAL
ILLUPPAIKURICHCHI
MUKKUDAI
SATTUPPATTU
ATTALANALLUR

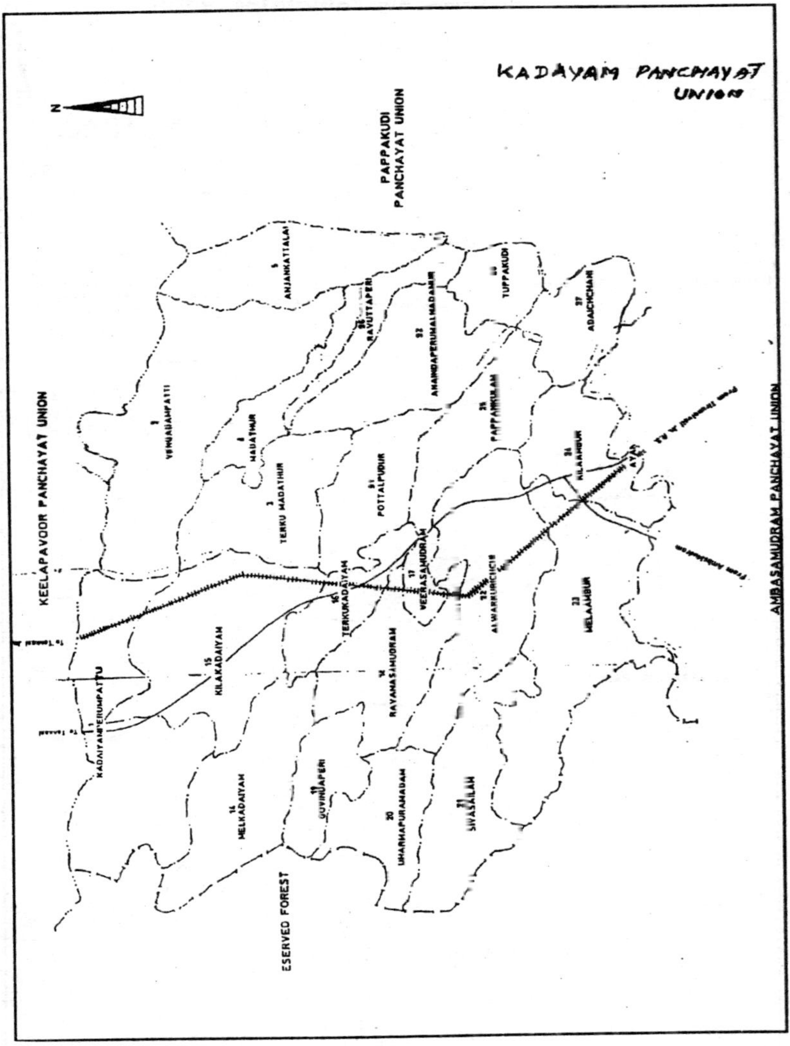
KADAYAM PANCHAYAT UNION
PAPPAKUDI PANCHAYAT UNION
KEELAPAVOOR PANCHAYAT UNION
AMBASAMUDRAM PANCHAYAT UNION
ESERVED FOREST
ANJANKATTALAI
TUPPAKUDI
ADAICHCHANI
RAVUTTAPERI
ANANDAPERUMALNADANUR
PAPPANKULAM
TERKU MADATHUR
POTTALPUDUR
KILAAMBUR
VEERASAMUDRAM
TERKUKADAIYAM
KILAKADAIYAM
RAYAMASAMUDRAM
MELAAMBUR
MELKADAIYAM
SIVASAILAM

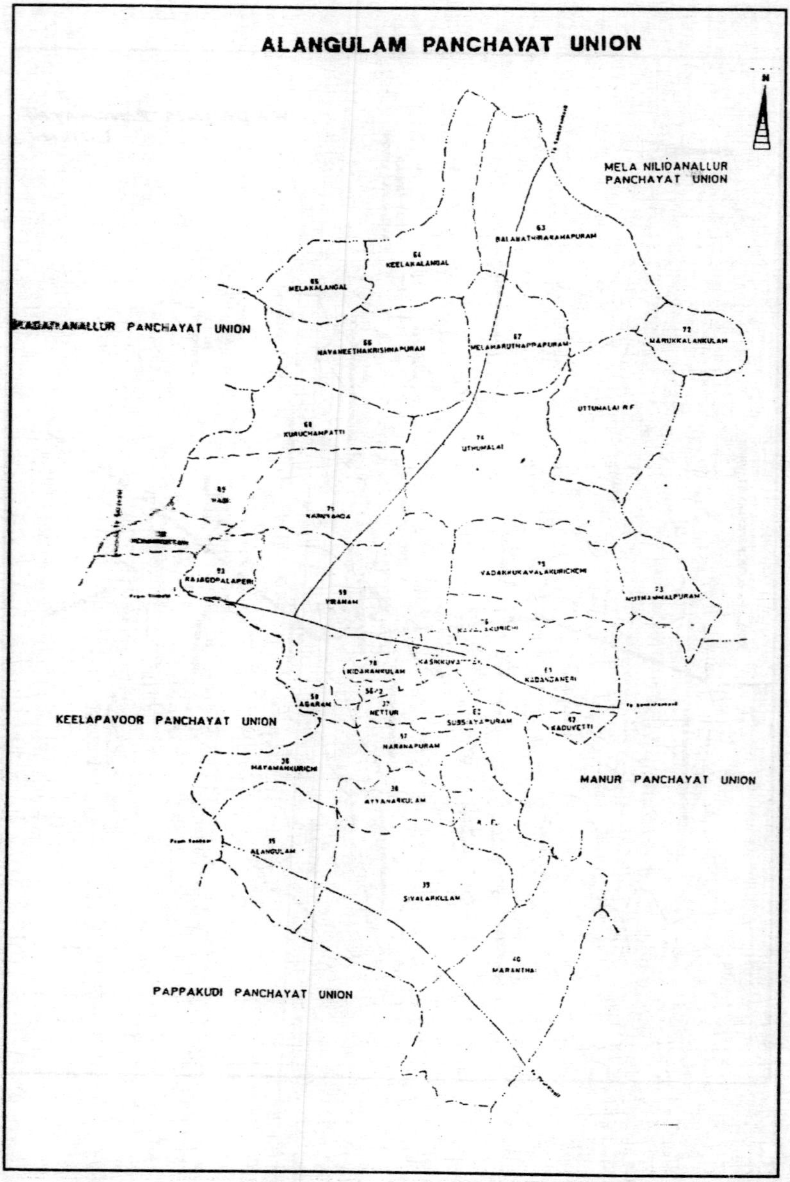
ALANGULAM PANCHAYAT UNION
N
MELA NILIDANALLUR PANCHAYAT UNION
PANCHAYAT UNION
KEELAPAVOOR PANCHAYAT UNION
MANUR PANCHAYAT UNION
PAPPAKUDI PANCHAYAT UNION
BALANATHIRARAMAPURAM
KEELAKALANGAL
MELAKALANGAL
NAVANEETHAKRISHNAPURAM
MELAMARUTHAPPAPURAM
MARUKKALANKULAM
UTTUMALAI R.F.
KURUCHAMPATTI
UTHUMALAI
VADAKKUKAVALAKURICHCHI
RAJAGOPALAPERI
VIRANAM
KIDARANKULAM
KADANGANERI
AGARAM
NETTUR
SUBBAIYAPURAM
KADUVETTI
NARANAPURAM
MAYAMANKURICHI
AYYANARKULAM
R.F.
ALANGULAM
SIVALARKULAM
MARANTHAI

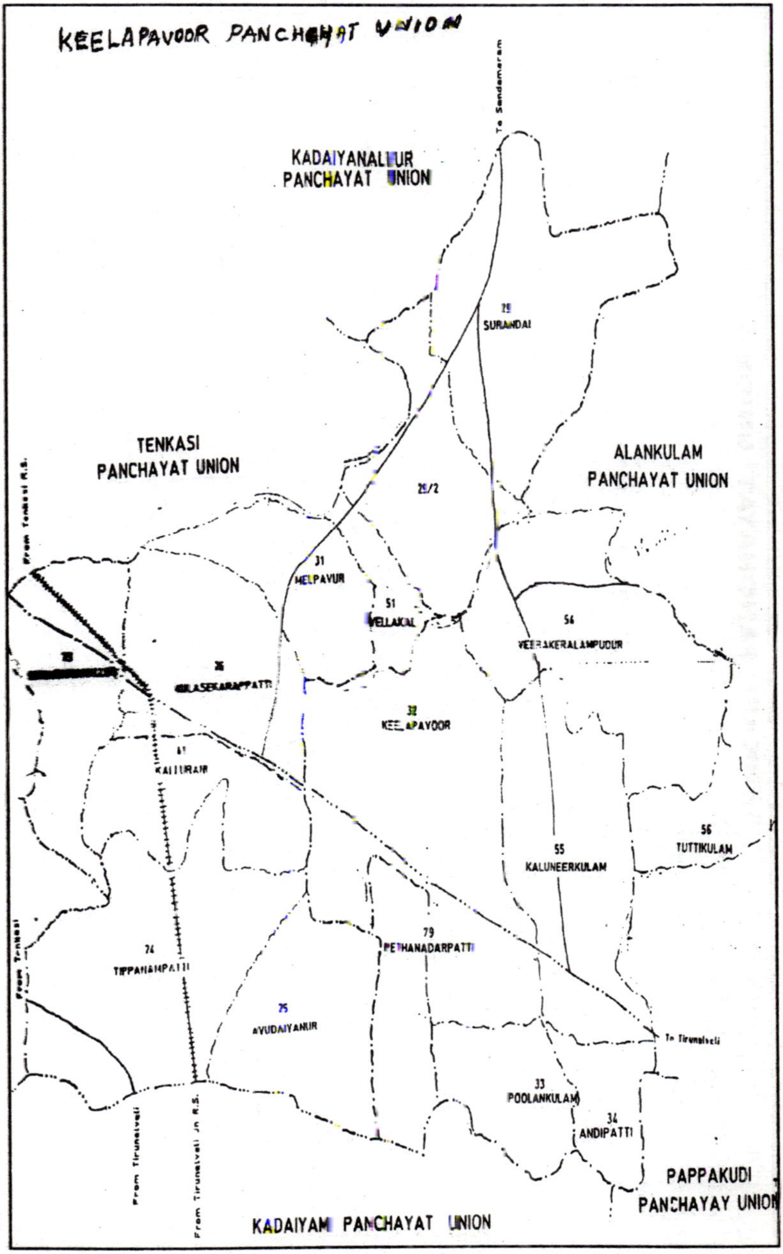
KEELAPAVOOR PANCHAYAT UNION
To Sendamaram
KADAIYANALLUR
PANCHAYAT UNION
SURANDAI
TENKASI
PANCHAYAT UNION
ALANKULAM
PANCHAYAT UNION
From Tenkasi R.S.
29/2
31
MELPAVUR
51
VELLAKAL
56
VEERAKERALAMPUDUR
32
KEELAPAVOOR
KALLURANI
56
TUTTIKULAM
55
KALUNEERKULAM
From Tenkasi
79
PETHANADARPATTI
74
TIPPANAMPATTI
25
AVUDAIYANUR
To Tirunelveli
33
POOLANKULAM
34
ANDIPATTI
From Tirunelveli
From Tirunelveli Jn R.S.
PAPPAKUDI
PANCHAYAY UNION
KADAIYAM PANCHAYAT UNION

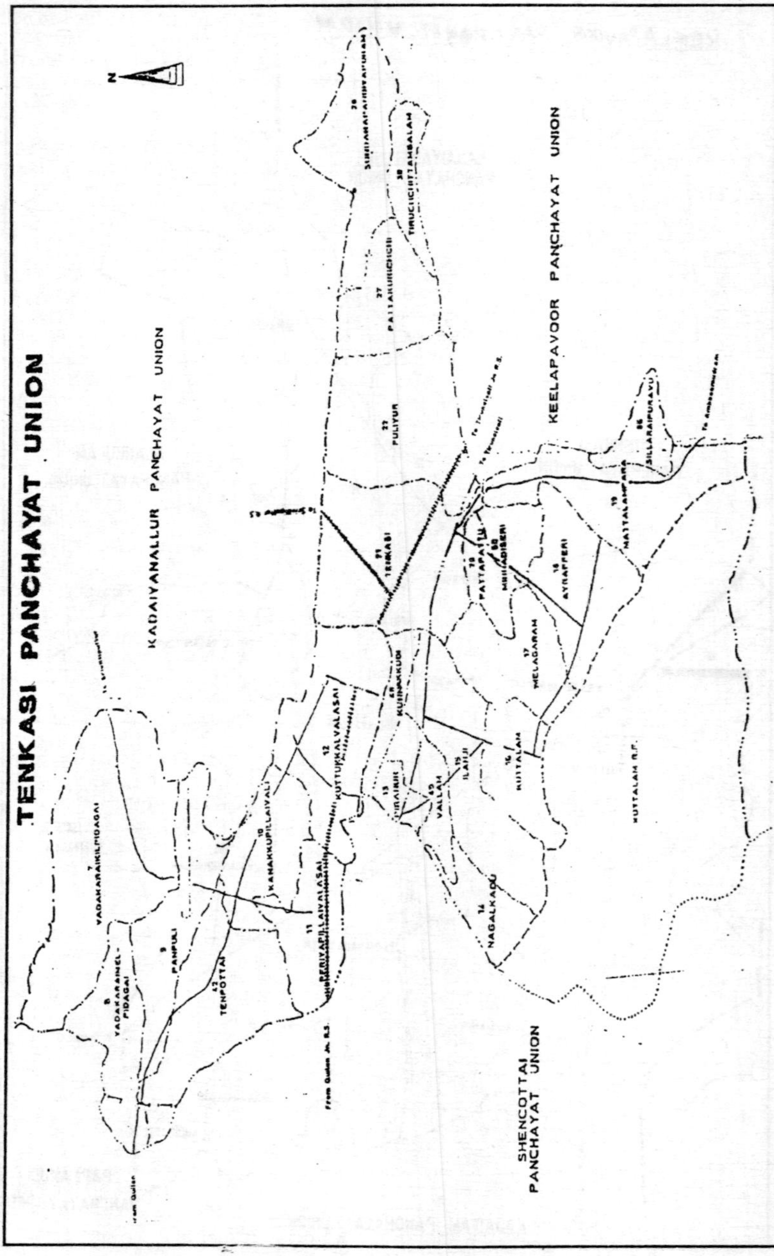
TENKASI PANCHAYAT UNION
KADAIYANALLUR PANCHAYAT UNION
KEELAPAVOOR PANCHAYAT UNION
SHENCOTTAI PANCHAYAT UNION
TENKASI
PULIYUR
PANPULI
TENPOTTAI
VALLAM
KUTTALAM
MELAGARAM
AYRAPPERI
NAGALKADU
KUTTALAM R.F.

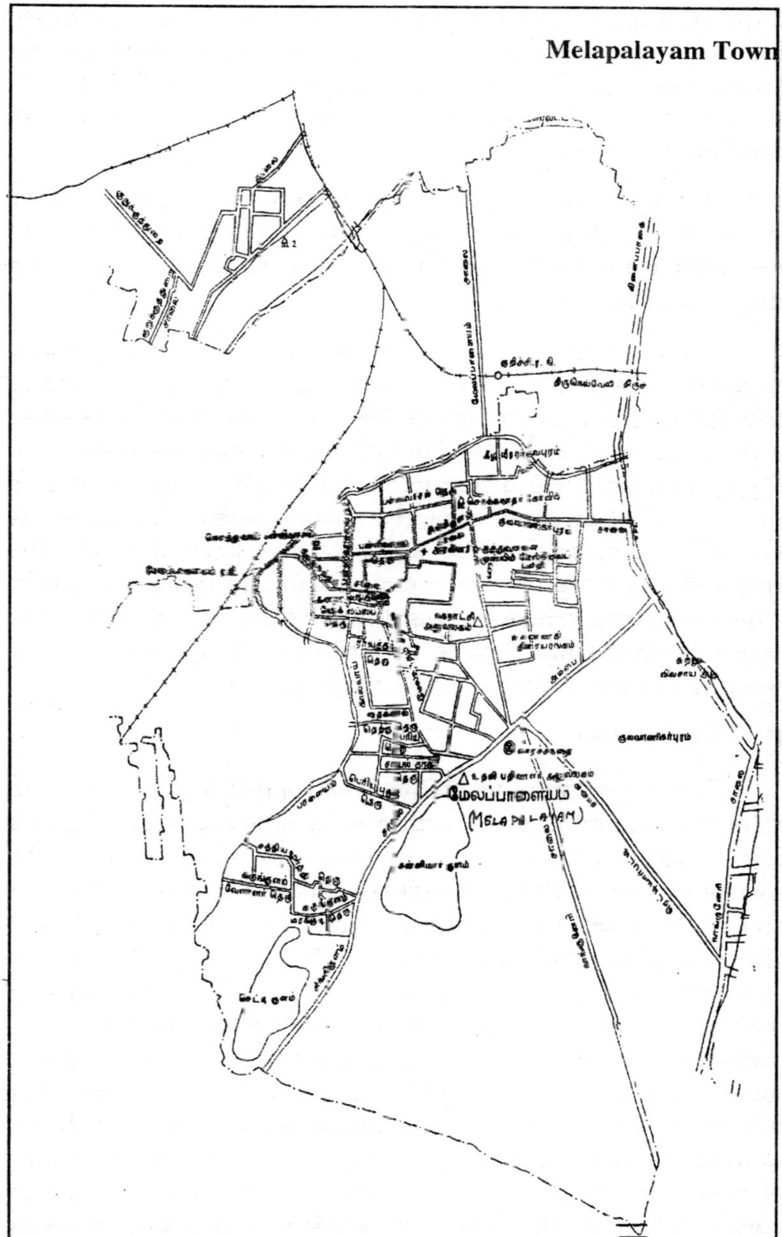
Melapalayam Town
மேலப்பாளையம்

a questionnaire. The questions in these sections were based on the objectives of the study. Most questions in the Interview-schedule were in the form of interrogative statements, and to all the questions a set of alternative answers was given.

A pre-test schedule was administered to 25 respondents. It was restructured with some additions and deletions. The modified schedule prepared thus was used as a tool to collect data from the respondents.

Field work for the present study was carried out personally by the researcher. The survey was conducted in several stages from December 1995 to October 1996 covering a time period of 9 moths. Though the interview-schedule for the respondents was constructed in English, it was translated into Tamil while conducting the survey because Tamil is the regional language. The suggestions provided by the respondents were also recorded at the end of the schedule. The completed schedules were field-verified immediately in order to avoid any lapses and the resultant revisits was seeking clarifications from the respondents.

II. Observations

The observation technique was applied to collect certain relevant data in order to facilitate the study. Certain delicate issues were avoided by a careful administration of the interview-schedule. Through observation the researcher could understand the working conditions, the pressures on the working children imposed by their parents and contractors, the seriousness of the health problems of working children, legal measures and the like. In this work, certain pertinent information gained by observation method have been included in appropriate places. The researcher being an inhabitant of the study area, his first hand knowledge of the child beedi workers and his observations of several activities of these workers in the area were also useful to the study. However, assistance of other persons such as village level workers was also sought to establish rapport with the village, wherever possible and necessary.

III. Case-Study

In addition to these tools of data collection, case-study method was also used to collect detailed information from experienced child workers, parents and contractors who were capable of giving certain interesting and relevant information. This has, directly or indirectly, supported certain observations made in the field. In addition to this, a few less experienced children were also interviewed and treated as case-studies because they were more spontaneous. This qualitative information has enriched the study in several ways.

IV. Collection of Secondary Data

Various publications and reports were collected from the Ministry of Labour New Delhi, V.V. Giri National Labour Institute Noida, United Nations Children Education Fund (UNICEF) offices New Delhi & Chennai, National Institute of Public Co-operation and Child Development (NIPCCD) office New Delhi, Ministry of Welfare New Delhi, Ministry of Rural Development New Delhi. Ministry of Law New Delhi. International Labour Organisation (International Labour Organisation) Branch offices New Delhi & Chennai, Indian Council of Social Science Research (ICSSR) Documentation Centre New Delhi, Institute of Labour Studies Chennai Madras Institute of Developmental Studies, Chennai, and other University libraries.

In addition to this, discussions were also held and views shared with the leaders of Beedi Workers' Association, officials of non-Government organisations, Labour offices, Tirunelveli District CACL (Campaign Against Child Labour) Board Members, District Child Labour Elimination Project officer, Local Body Administrators and District Collector. Other researchers who conducted similar studies in the area were also consulted.

DATA PROCESSING AND ANALYSIS

After the field work, the filled-up schedules were carefully scrutinised and edited in order to ensure accuracy, consistency and completeness. The coding of data was done manually by the researcher. The classification, tabulation and further statistical treatment of data were computerised. The data were qualitative and quantitative in nature. The qualitative data were converted into percentage. Most of the analyses were based on the responses presented in the form of frequency tables. The data thus tabulated were systematically processed and interpreted on the basis of the objectives formulated. These interpretations have been carefully studied and conclusions were drawn.

Most of the analyses were based on the simple and relevant statistical tools such as percentages and averages. In addition to this, data were analysed by using appropriate statistical techniques, especially Chi-Square test to examine the significance of the association between the variables taken for the analysis.

LIMITATIONS OF THE STUDY

Every research study suffers from constraints and limitations. While some of these are inherent in the research design, some others become part of the study during various stages of operations. The present study consists of the following constraints and limitations:

(i) This thesis has limited its scope to the study of child labour in beediworks only.

(ii) It is limited to certain areas where there is high concentration of child labour in Tirunelveli District in Tamil Nadu.

(iii) It has limited the study to full time non-schooling child labourers in beediworks.

(iv) It has also limited the number of samples to 500 for facilitating an in-depth study.

Despite these limitations, the study has a solid evidence based on the responses from child labourers in the beediworks. Based on the findings, the study researcher has out with valid inferences and concrete suggestions.

SCHEME OF PRESENT RESEARCH REPORT

The present study has branched off into 7 ramifications as detailed below:

The first chapter captioned Introduction and Design of the Study gives a terse account of the statement of the problem, importance of the study, objectives of the study, operational definition of the concepts, methodology, sampling design, limitations of the study and the organisation of the research report.

Chapter II entitled *Review of Literature* deals with reviews of various related works and the uniqueness of the present study.

Chapter III, *Socio-Demographic Profile of Working Children* presents the variations among the child workers with respect to variables such as sex, age, religion, education, size of the family of the child workers, income, rural/urban background, process of beediworks, years of experience and place of work.

Chapter IV titled *Levels of Exploitation* discusses the cause(s) for the presence of so many child workers in the beedi industry and analyses the various ways in which these child workers are exploited by their parents and contractors.

Chapter V entitled *Laws Relating to Child Labour* examines legislation relating to children, reports of various committees and the Supreme Court verdict.

Chapter VI, *Health Problems*, presents a general appraisal of the occupational diseases, dietary system and physical atmosphere.

The final chapter of the research report, *Conclusion*, gives a critical account of the major findings of the study and also provides suitable suggestions and recommendations to tackle the problem of child labour.

REFERENCES

1. Parveen Nangia, *Child Labour Cause-Effect Syndrome* (New Delhi: Janak Publishers, 1987), p. 7.

2. Ibid.

3. K.P,. Kangle, *The Kautilya Arthasashtra, Part II,* (University of Bombay, 1963), pp. 271-274.

4. Gerry Rodgers and Guy Standing, "Economic Roles of Children in Low Income Countries". *International Labour Review* 120 (January-February 1981): 12.

5. A.N. Sadu and Amerjit Singh, "Children Labour in India" *The Indian Worker* 29 (October 1980): 61.

6. Peter Burke, "The Child in the World of Yesterday", *Ekistics: The Problem and Science of Human Settlements:* 45 (272) (September-October 1978): 376.

7. Enid Schildkrout, "The Employment of Children in Kano (Nigeria)", in Gerry Rodgers and Guy Standing, eds., *Child Work, Poverty and Underdevelopment,* International Labour Organisation, Geneva, 1981, p. 95.

8. Smithu Kothari, "Child Labour in Sivakasi", *Economic and Politically Weekly* 2 (July 1983): 119.

9. J. Christopher Daniel, "Child Worker has come to stay", *Social Welfare* 14 (November 1976): 6.

10. Ibid.

11. Anna Davin, "Children Labour: The Working Class Family and Domestic Ideology in 19th Century Britain", *Development and Change* 13 (November 1982): 640-641.

12. J. Christopher Daniel, "Child Worker has come to stay", *Social Welfare* 14 (November 1976): 6.

13. Sandor Komoloski, "Changes in Hungarian Families" *Ekistics: The Problem and Science of Human Settlements* 45 (September-October 1978: 369.

14. Subrat Kumar Sing Deo, "Child Labour: A Collosal Misuse of Human Resource", in R.N. Pati, *Rehabilitation of Child Labourers in India* (New Delhi: Ashish Publishign House, 1991), p. 265.

15. Braja Mohan Otta, "Child Labour—As an adjunct to domestic mode of production", in R.N. Pati, *Rehabilitation of Child Labourers in India*, p. 196.

16. V.V. Giri, *Labour Problem in Indian Industry* (New Delhi: Asia Publishing House, 1960), p. 360.

17. Jinesh Chandra Kulshreshtha, *Child Labour in India* (New Delhi: Ashish Publishing House, 1978), p. 2.

18. *Encyclopaedia of Social Sciences,* Vol. III, Macmillan Company, New York, 1930, pp. 412-413.

19. *Child Labour: Extract from the Report of the Director-General to the International Labour Conference, 69th Session, 1983,* p. 6.

20. Ibid.

21. Gurupadasamy Committee Report on Child Labour, 1979 as cited by Gerry Rodgers and Guy Standing, eds., *Child Work, Poverty and Underdevelopment* (Geneva: International Labour Organisation, 1981), pp. 10-11.

22. Stephen B. Wood, *"Constitutional Politics in the Progressive Era: Child Labour and the Law"* (Chicago: The University of Chicago Press, 1968), p. 8.

23. Rajani Kanta Das, *Child Labour in India* (Geneva: International Labour Organisation, 1934), p. 6.

24. K.K. Misra, "Dimensions of Child Labour in India", in Pati, *Rehabilitation of Child Labourers in India,* p. 145.

25. Jinesh Chandra Kulshreshtha *Child Labour in India,* p. 2.

26. E. Stein and J. Davis, *Labour Problems in America* (New York: Farror and Rinchart Inc., 1940), pp. 112-113.

27. I.S. Singh, *Child Labour* (New Delhi: Oxford and IBH Publishing Co. Pvt. Ltd., 1992), p. 7.

28. Braja Mohan Otta, "Child Labour-As and Adjunct to Domestic mode of Production", In Pati, *Rehabilitation of Child Labourers in India*, p. 196.

29. D.A. Naidu, "Some Micro-determinants of Child Labour in Rural South India: A Provisional Analysis (Paper presented at a seminar on *Child Labour and Health* organised jointly by Tata Institute of Social Science and World Health Organisation, Bombay, 1982).

30. N.K. Bhura and B.K. Behera, "Incidence of Child Labour in Orissa: Case Studies from Bhubaneshwar", in Pati *Rehabilitation of Child Labourers in India,* p. 120.

31. P.V. Gopujkar and V.S. Dhole, "A Summary of the Study of Working Children in Tribal Area of Maharashtra" (Paper presented at a seminar on *Child Labour and Health),* p. 1082.

32. Swapan Kumar Sinha, *Child Labour in Calcutta: A Sockiological Study* (Calcutta: N.P. Sale (P) Ltd., 1991), p. 10.

33. Kishi Kumar, *Definition, Concept and Overview of Child Labour* (A Paper presented at a workshop organised by National Institute of Public Co-operation and Child Development, New Delhi, 1995).

34. Nalini Sekar and Suresh Rao, "Perspective Paper on Causes of Child Labour" (Paper Presented at a Workshop, on *Causes and Prevention of Child Labour in South Asian Countries,* Organised by Campaign Against Child Labour, Central Secretariat, Bombay, 1996.

35. R.S. Goyal, "Problems of Child Labour in India", in Pati, *Rehabilitation of Child Labourers in India,* p. 153.

36. *Convention on the Rights of the Child: World Declaration and Plan of Action from the World Summit for Children,* United Nations Children Education Fund (India Country Office, 1991), p. 20.

37. G. Karunanithi, *Child Labour in Beedi Industry in Tirunelveli-Kattabomman District of Tamil Nadu,* (A Project Report submitted to the Union Ministry of Labour, Government of India, 1995), p. 4.

38. *Convention on the Rights of the Child,* p. 58.

39. Elias Mendelievich, "Introduction", *Children at Work,* (Geneva: International Labour Organisation, 1979), p. 4.

40. Karunanithi, *"Children Labour in Beedi Industry",* p. 50.

41. K.G. Gangrade, 'India', *Children at Work,* eds., Elias Mendelievich, p. 81.

42. A. Dharmalingam, "Female Beedi Workers in a South Indian Village", *Economic and Political Weekly,* 12 (July 1993): 146.

43. Neera Burra, *Born to Work* (Bombay: Oxford University Press, 1995), pp. 231-236.

44. *Report of the Director General, International Labour Conference, 69th Session* (Geneva: International Labour Organisation, 1983), p. 16.

45. Gerry Rodgers and Guy Standing, "The Economic Roles of Children: Issues for Analysis", in *Child Work, Poverty and Underdevelopment,* eds., in Rodgers and Standing, (Geneva: International Labour Organisation, 1981), p. 8.

46. *Report of the Committee on Child Labour* (Government of India; Minsitry of Labour, 1979), p. 8.

47. Jan Videk, "World's Working Children Need Protection Against Exploitation", *Eastern Economist* 18 (October 1978): 822-823.

48. *Child Labour: What is to be done?* (Document for Discussion at the Informal Tripartite Meeting at the Ministerial Level), Geneva: International Labour Organisation, 12th June 1996, p. 4.

49. Mahaveer Jain, Elimination of Child Labour in India: The Government Initiative (Noida: V.V. Giri National Labour Institute, 1996), p. 1.

50. *The Hindu*, March 4, 1997, p. 14.

51. G. Karunanithi, *Child Labour in North Arcot Ambedkar District: An in-depth study of Pledged Children in Beediworks* (Project report submitted to the Indian Council of Social Science Research, New Delhi, 1993), p. 16.

52. *Report on Occupational Health Issues of Women in the Unorganised Sector,* (New Delhi: The National Commission of Self-Employed Women, 1988), p. 156.

53. Karunanithi, *Child Labour in North Arcot Ambedkar District,* p. 16.

54. *Indian Express,* December 9, 1992, p. 9.

2

Review of Literature

There are about 21 countries in the Western and Southern parts of Africa where the proportion of child labour is in the ratio of 35 per thousand and in certain parts the proportion is 50 per thousand. The countries outside Africa which are included in this category are Haiti from the Caribbean, and Nepal, Bhutan, Bangladesh and Sri Lanka from Asia. Some of the Asian countries like Syria. Lebanon, Jordan, Saudi Aribia, Yemen and Malaysia have a lower proportion of child labour which is reported to be 5-15 per thousand population. In the European countries like North America and Australia, the proportion of child labour is very low. The ratio of child labour seems to be far more negligible in Iraq, Quwait, Singapore and Japan. It is reported that a negligible proportion of working children are found in Russia, Newzealand and America. Of the whole child labour in the world, one-third (10-14 years) are in rural areas and one-eighth in the urban centers in India.[1]

Although various commissions like the Child Labour Commission 1954, National Commission on Labour 1969, and Report of the Committee on Child Labour popularly known as Gurupadaswamy Report 1979, have very strongly condemned the non-fulfilment of constitutional provisions which protect the rights of children, a National Institute of Public Co-operation and Children Development (NIPCCD) Report (1977) of the Committee on Employment of Children in India and the findings of a seminar organised by National Institute of Public Co-operation and Children Development

(NIPCCDZ) (1982) on Child and Law, have revealed that the shameful act of child labour is still persisting in the country and particularly in un-organised sectors. Besides the various reports of the commissions as mentioned above, a good number of research studies all over the country, have been conducted on the factors associated with child labour, like working conditions, health measures, legal intervention on child labour and other related aspects. But, there has been very little research work done on the child labour in beedi industry. Though many aspects of child labour have been studied extensively, exploitation and legal intervention on child labour are mostly unexplored areas. A large number of children are engaged in brick-kilns in Rajasthan, gem polishing factories in Jaipur, zari embroiding work in Lucknow, metal work in Moradabad and the like.The summary review of studies on child workers in these sectors, have brought to light the age, conditions and duration and finally the paltry returns they get from their employers.[2]

Another interesting study on child labour in Bangalore city has been reported by Krishna Kumari. Bangalore, now a growing cosmopolitan city with temperate climate for all the twelve months, remained one of the favourite places of the British rulers. People from different parts of the country, have migrated to Bangalore in search of better avenues. Among the migrants, there are labourers who have thronged to this city, because of employment opportunities in the labour market. With the influx of labourers, thousands of juggies and slums have come up in the outskirts of this city. The overall finding of this study revealed that the drop-out rate among boys was more than that of girls. While a survey on the occupation of the parents of these children was conducted, it was found that 16 per cent of them are not employed, 84 per cent are engaged in part-time manual/ non-manual work. On an average, it is observed that the children's contribution to the family income works out to be 19 per cent. In some families, children contribute a major portion of money to the family income. As regards the housing of the child workers, most of the hutments are small, dark and dreary, two rooms of squalor and dirt. When asked about depriving their children of education, the parents said that education was only a means to an end and since their children had a job, there was no need for education.[3]

D.A. Naidu conducted a study entitled "Micro-Determinants of children labour: an evidence from rural south India". The main variables considered by this investigation were caste, father's education and occupation, economic status, perceived economic value and occupational and educational aspirations of children and modernisation. The findings revealed that only 23 per cent of children, in the age group of 5-9 years, were working as against 77 per cent of elder children in the age group of 10-14 years. The second revelation of this study was that the number of working girls was greater than the number of working boys. With regard to education, more younger children than the elders and more boys than girls had attended schools. The educational aspirations of their children were in line with the education of their fathers. The degree of children labour was in line with the degree of economic need of the family.[4]

In her survey of child labour in Tamil Nadu, Savithiri states that poverty, large family, death of the bread winner, physical and mental illness of parents or unemployment of adult members in the family are some of the reasons which contribute to the existence of child labour. The author mentions that in the rural areas of Tamil Nadu, agriculture and animal husbandry are the main sectors which engage child labour. Regarding the working conditions stated by the author, a majority of the children are employed without any fixed wages. She discloses that, in the city of Madras, anti-social elements train children as smugglers, beggars and even as pimps. Although the Government of Tamil Nadu has introduced free mid-day meals for children besides provisions for uniform, books and equipment, still the parents from lower and middle class families prefer to employ their children rather than send them to school. As a result, thousands of tender children are pushed into the market of uneducated child workers.[5]

Khandekar's study is enlightening as to the situation of children and youth who are employed in various establishments in Great Mumbai. The study reveals that the low-economic status of the family, migration from rural areas to Mumbai, are some of the main factors that force the children to join the crowd of Mumbai's labour market. Lack of education happens to be the second largest factor for the children taking to labour. The study also observes that a large number of children in this area have been forced to supplement the family income. Another group of children state that they work in order to have economic independence.[6]

The Indian Council of Child Welfare has conducted a study on "Working Children in Delhi". And it brings to light the fact that most of the children in Delhi are working in the automobile workshops. Dhabas, tea-stalls and in domestic services. Some children are engaged in rag picking and shoe-shining. The report further shows that the working conditions of the children are unhygienic and pitiable. The wages of the child workers in Delhi vary from according to the type of job, place of work, age of the children and economic condition of their parents. Those child labourers who do not have any place of shelter in Delhi spend all the 24 hours at their work sites and as a result, they work for twelve hours a day. Some of them have to work near furnaces, where the temperature is at melting point, and these children even risk their lives.[7]

Pati and Swain have conducted a study on child labourers in Bhubaneswar city. Their study is an attempt to assess the social life of street children in the city of Bhubaneswar. The study discloses that more than 65 per cent of the working children are in the age group of 14-16 years and 34 per cent in the age group below 14 years. They are working in canteens and restaurants, garages, various small shops and construction sites. Regarding the working hours of these children, it varies from 6 to 10 hours a day and similarly the monthly salary of these child labourers varies from Rs. 100 to 300. The children working in construction sites have reported that their working conditions are rather conductive, but they are satisfied with the wages. With respect to their health condition, many of them are suffering from gastro-intestinal discorders and skin diseases.[8]

Nath and Majumdar have studied the status of the working children in Calcutta. The investigators found that 36.7 per cent of the children had lost their fathers, 11.5 per cent had lost their mothers and 2.3 per cent had lost both parents. The children had an average working age of 9.8 years. A majority of the children had never attended school.[9]

Mir has shown his concern towards child labour in the organised sector, particularly in the handicraft and carpet weaving centers. It needs to be mentioned that the child labourers are not directly in the pay-roll of the government but helping their parents who are employed in these centers. The author has further established that poverty, illiteracy and adult unemployment are the other factors contributing to this menace. The author has shown that a majority of the children and their parents represent the economically as well as socially backward pockets of the society.[10]

N.A. Shah has conducted a study on child labour in an unorganised sector in Kashmir. The overall analysis of data unveils the fact that inadequate income, illiteracy and ignorance of parents in addition to the large family size are the precipitating factors which drag young ones in to the world of labour. Physical deformities and weak eye sight are the effects of child labour.[11]

A.N. Singh, in his study entitled "Child Labour in India: A Socio-Economic Perspective", discusses in detail various reasons for child labour in India. Child labour in various areas and fields need sympathetic attention and statutory provisions. He concludes that the practice of child labour is primarily found among the economically weaker sections of society. The working conditions of child labour in the carpet weaving industry are grossly detrimental to their growth and development. The child workers are even deprived of the minimum requirements that are available to their counterparts in the organised sectors. The socio-economical backwardness of the children makes them vulnerable to exploitation in the carpet weaving industry. Abolition of child labour is not favoured by empoloyers and parents for economic reasons. The carpet weaving industry has no socio-political awareness.[12]

The National Commission of Labour (1969) reports that the gradual reduction in the employment of child labour since Independence is due to the expansion of educational facilities by the state and, also, to a sterner enforcement of statutory provision relating to child labour. Employment of children is almost non-existence in organised sectors such as small plantations, restaurants and hotels, cotton gaining, stone breaking, carpet weaving, brick kilns, handicrafts and road making. Employment of under aged child workers is also reported to be continuing in certain remote rural areas where enforcement of statutory provision is more difficult.[13]

A 1930 of the Royal Commission on Labour in India, observes, inter alia, that the most noteworthy effect of the 1922 Act was that the employment of children in mills, weaving and cotton spinning industries had reduced. In its occasional references to the working conditions of children, the report mentions that "children usually work five hours a day without any interval... In the smaller factories, hours of work are often long and their machinery is unfenced and sanitation too, is often defective". It is also reported that section 26 of the Indian Mines Act, 1923, under which no child could be employed in a mine, has caused some hardship. Poverty, invariably, induces most of the parents to make their children work. In the opinion of the Bombay Textile Labour Union on the employment of children, as mentioned in the Royal Commission's Report, the maximum age limit for the employment of children should be raised from twelve to fourteen years. The employment of children in factories before eight in the morning and after five in the evening should be prohibited.[14]

The Labour Investigation Committee, appointed by the Government of India, collected, in 1946 data relating to wages and earnings, employment and housing, and social conditions of labour in India. The Committee investigated the risks which bring about insecurity, the need to meet such risks through labour and the methods suitable to meet them and the housing and factory conditions. It is observed that the problem was non-existence in large factories. However, it continued in mica splitting, shellac, beedi making, carpet weaving, glass and other small industries. The Committee found that, little girls are employed n Kerala State in the spinning section of the cotton textile industry, while in Kashmir children of five or six years work in carpet weaving. The children are employed because the income of the family needs supplementing, and the lack of educational facilities would make children idle if they do not join the labour force. The Committee feels that, it is not enough to merely prohibit the employment of children, but it is essential to adopt simultaneously positive measures to wean away child labour from industrial employment. With a view to protect the future generation, the Committee emphasizes the fulfillment of legal provisions with careful inspection and the sanctioning of educational and other facilities to the children.[15]

National Commission on Labour, was appointed in 1969, by the Ministry of Labour, Employment and Rehabilitation, to review the conditions of labour and suggest measures for their improvement. The Commission found that in certain industries such as glass, beedi, carpet manufacturing and so forth the conditions in which children work were deplorable. It disclosed that the employment of children was more of an economic problem than anything else. The Commission reported that early employment resulted in the denial of education to children. Therefore, it suggested that the working hours for the children should be restricted so as to enable them to attend school. Where the number of children is adequate, the employers with the assistance of the State governments, should make arrangements to combine work with education.[16]

Harban Singh Committee which investigated "the problems of child labour in various factories and industries in Ramanathapuram district of Tamil Nadu", feels that child labour is one of the most crucial factors in the development of the match and fireworks industries in Ramanathapuram area. A community of shared interests has evolved as a result of constant interaction between the employers and employees and this is in turn results in the increasing employment of children. The government agencies have also been partly responsible for perpetrating this miserable state of child labour. The Committee report suggests that the working hours should be reduced, wages should be increased and instead of the prevailing piece-rate system, the wages should be linked to the cost of living index. It also recommends that non-formal education should be given to children in the factories. School attendance should be made compulsory and it should be a precedent condition for employment in factories. However, the various recommendations suggest that the radical measures should be taken to end the scourge of child labour.[17]

Report of the Committee on Child Labour 1979, details the causes leading to and the problems arising out of the employment of children in India. The Committee investigates the dimensions of child labour and the occupations in which children are employed and the adequacy and implementation of the existing laws. It highlights the condition of child labour in beedi manufacturing and glass bangle industry, handloom and carpet weaving industry, gem polishing industry, and in domestic works, hotels machine tools and repair shops. Children start working in these industries at the age of seven or eight. The full extent of their exploitation can be comprehended by findings such as the young diamond cutters developing eye defects very soon. Moreover, the diamond cutters are dismissed mercilessly from their jobs as soon as the nearly signs of eye fatigue are detected by the employers. The Committee emphasizes, that there is a need for a single model legislation on child labour in India, so that there are no anomalies on the issues like minimum wages, working hours, medical examination, penalties for offences, etc. It has been suggested that the minimum age for entry into the workforce be fixed as fifteen years. It also stresses the need to involve social workers, voluntary organisations and trade unions as well as parents to facilitate the enforcement of legislative measures.[18]

The 1981 report of Child Labour in Indian Industries, presents the various aspects of child labour, i.e., employment, wages and earnings, working conditions and welfare facilities. It was found that in most factories the hours of work, as prescribed under the Act were not being strictly adhered to. Children of very tender age were found working in certain industries, such as beedimaking, matchworks, handloom fishing, hotels and restaurants and repair shops. The Report states that a majority of working children come from poor families to supplement their family income. They are compelled to discontinue their studies as there is no provision of night schools for those who want to continue studies. The Report stresses the need to bring about a change in the social attitude towards child labour, besides the tightening of laws and activating the enforcement machinery.[19]

Ramesh Kanbargi, in his study of "Child labour in the Indian Sub-continent: Dimensions and Implications", discusses in detail the monetisation of the rural economy, stagnation in wage rates and declining employment opportunities for children that affect the economic value of children in rural areas. The increasing expenditure involved in the schooling of children — 3 although schooling is free, the expenditure on school going children is substantial in terms of clothing, books and stationery—adds to the economic stress in the family. Thus, a situation has risen where, for a majority, the wealth flow is from the parents to the children. Consequently, what has so far induced the drive for high fertility has weakened. It has been argued by many that a decline in the net value of children will reduce the family size ideals and people will resort to fertility regulations.[20]

B. Chakravarthy finds that the causes of drop-out and stagnation in elementary education in India are not only economic but also social and educational. This analysis suggests that urbanisation, levels of development and access to schools are important for a rapid rise in the level of literacy: they help promote the level of literacy by enhancing the number of enrollments in schools and by reducing drop-out rates. As a larger proportion of children enter into adulthood with minimum years of schooling, literacy rates show improvement. The study concludes that the rate of drop-our is much higher among Scheduled Castes and Scheduled Tribes and that it is the highest in the cause of girls belonging to these communities. The proportion of children reaching class VII is very low at middle school level because the children of that age-group are more prone to child labour. The study then seeks to clarify the broad dimensions of child labour in the field of agriculture and non-agriculture as evidenced from census and other surveys. This is followed by a review of studies on child labour being an impediment to universalisation of elementary education and literacy in Andhra Pradesh.[21]

Ivy George, in her study on "Child Labour and Child Work", concludes that the children's participation in the handloom industry at Chinnallipatti is a positive experience which contributes in various ways to the development of the children as well as their community. She discusses some possible directions in which, with a change of strategies, different restructured production environment can be achieved. Attention is called to changes necessary in educational and health facilities, better services from the town panchayat and issues relating to the existence and maintenance of the handloom industry. She explains how the industry affects the children of Chinnallipathi. And she questions whether it has been possible to identify work and labour that are in operation and whether it is possible to transform labour settings into work settings and if such a transformation is possible, how it can be brought about.[22]

A.F. Ferguson and Company conducted at study on "Child Labour in Fireworks". The main findings of this study are: awareness of the use of child labour in the fireworks is quite high because of the media like newspapers, magazines and movies. More than half of the respondents felt that child labour in any sector is bad and should be stopped while almost two-thirds felt that child labour in the fire cracker industry in particular should be stopped. This study discloses that a majority of the respondents in Madras feel that nothing can be achieved without first settling the problem of poverty. Higher income and educated groups feel strongly that child labour is wrong and can be eliminated only by government's stringent measures. A majority of the respondents are willing to destroy the evil of child labour.[23]

D. Jayaraj in his research paper explores the relevance of distress as the determinant of labour force participation of women and children. Distress, the major determinant of labour force participation of women and children, has three dimensions, viz., level of income, distribution of income and stability of income or earnings. Identification or classification of the three dimensions of distress offers a convenient framework for analyzing the impact of various factors that determine the participation of women and children in the labour force. Apart from factors related to distress, to capture the impact of sociological factors, the percentage of Scheduled Caste population in the total population has been introduced into the analysis. The analysis of the paper indicates that distribution of income and stability in earnings are the major determinants of labour force participation of women and children. These results indicate the fallacy in relying solely on raising the level of income or the general level of prosperity to eradicate distress. Thus, the paper argues for redistribution of resources, particularly land, as the most suited policy measures to eradicate poverty and thereby the distress-induced labour force participation of women and children, particularly children.[24]

G. Karunanithi in his report on the Status of Primary Education in Kovilpatti (Match block where match industry is concentrated) and Aruppukottai, (Feeder block, block from which children are recruited to match industry outside the feeder block) observes that the enrollment of children in the age group of 6-11 is higher in both blocks, but for girls it is relatively less. Drop-out rate is higher in the feeder block. Drop-out rate of girls is generally higher. More full-time child workers are employed in both blocks in the age group of 12-14. But, it is much more in the feeder block. There are more part-time workers in the match block. Girls perform in a poor way when compared to boys, but the ratio is more in terms of full time working children. Easy access to work in the match block has allowed the children to work part-time while attending school.[25]

Madras Institute of Develcpment Studies, has oriented itself towards an examination of the aspects of private costs incurred by the removal of child labour. On the demand side, the expected effect on total manufacturing cost of the possible increase in labour (and other) costs leads to the removal of child labour and on the supply side, the income foregone by the households presently provides child labour. Specifically, the study addresses the effects on the economics of manufacture that the removal of child labour may bring about and the modifications possible in the systems of manufacture, purchase of raw-material and marketing that is necessary to ensure industrial viability. The study also estimates the loss of income incurred by the households supplying child labour. The policy measures proposed by the study include mechanisation and alternative solutions, support of worker households; wage increase as an essential solution; and viability measure for the industry.[26]

Report of the Sub-Committee on Elimination of Child Labour in the Match and Fireworks Industries in Tamil Nadu, has provided detailed information on various aspects of child labour in match and fireworks industry in Sivakasi area of Tamil Nadu and has listed a feasible action plan for the elimination of child labour in phased manner. The recommendations of the Sub-Committee are in line with existing government policies regarding the support to intensive industries of labour which generate employment, as well as the protection of the small-scale and cottage sectors. This Committee has called for a integrated multi-sectorial approach, involving intervention in the industrial structure, household economy, education, communication and social mobilisation and enforcement, for the elimination of child labour. It has also recommend a corresponding administrative structure for implementing the action plan.[27]

The Supreme Court of India has reported the appalling conditions of the working children in the match belt. Recommendations of the Committee constituted by the Court are: packing should be done separately so that the children are not exposed to the chemicals inside the factory premises; employment of the children in fireworks should be stopped; State authorities should provide birth certificate to all children: and employers should be strictly directed to keep records of children employed. It is recommended that the piece-rate system be converted to time-rated wages and basic diet should be made available to the children in the factories, by the government or employer. All workers in the age group of 10-15 are to the insured against accidents. The employer has to pay Rs. 2 per worker per month towards welfare found. A permanent committee with a retired High Court Judge or a person of similar cadre should be set up to tackle the issue of child labour.[28]

M. Sumangala and B.S. Nagarajan conducted a study on "Economics of Child Labour and Fertility". This study has two parts: the first deals with child labour practice and the second discusses the fertility behaviour of the parents of child labour. The study concludes that the percentage share of female child workers to the total workforce is more than that of the male child workers in all the districts both rural and urban during all the three decades the study focuses upon. While male child workers' participation rate has showed a declining trend in all the districts during 1971 to 1981, female child workers' participation rate (both rural and urban) has increased in all districts during 1971 to 1981. An educated mother is found to be negatively related to fertility. The illiterate mothers have more children than those who are educated atleast upto middle school. Fertility among parents in joint families are higher than those in nuclear families. There exists a positive relationship between more number of children and practice of child labour in the study areas. Educational status of child labour shows that in almost all the cases, they are either non-starter illiterates or semi-illiterate drop-outs. At the aggregate level, as much as 72.5 per cent of child labourers are drop-outs from school and that too mostly at primary level. Not attending school has emerged as the fourth main reason reported for child labour by 39 per cent of mothers. Dropping out of school resulting in child labour, is found to be true in the study area.[29]

Department of Labour, Tamil Nadu gives a workshop report on the situation of working children in Tamilnadu. It is well said that if one wants to know a nation, one should look for it in its children. They are not only the future of any nation but also the strength in reserve for a nation. They are the crops which feed the future. If they are healthy and active, educated and informed and disciplined and trained the future of the action is well ensured. But, if they are lacking in the above aspects, a nation's future is doomed. Labour is workship, but it must be respected and extracted from those who are fit for it. And it is the duty of all the concerned employers, trade unions, society, government and voluntary organisations to achieve this objective.[30]

The Child Labour Cell of the National Labour Institute presents a report on child labour in the gem polishing industry in Jaipur. While dealing with the problem of child labour in gem polishing, the following considerations should be kept in mind: (i) if the gem artisan is in a position to look after the health and nutritional requirement of children and (ii) if he/she can send them to school, in case books and uniforms are provided free by the State. The State makes several allowances for the school-going children as it welcomes the growing awareness amongst parents of the importance of education. Parents, while the realise the importance of education, are also aware that the children work for several years without any wage or economic return and are only exploited for their cheap labour under the façade of apprenticeship for training in gem polishing. A mid-day meal programme for these schools can be an added attraction. An educated child entering the gem industry at the age of say, 15 years is better equipped to grasp and learn the skills needed and would definitely by in a better position to deal with the outside world. It is also recommended that vocational training in gem polishing, as an integral part of school work would motivate parents to educate their children. Incentives by way of loans, provision of raw material or purchase of finished goods should be given to the parents along with compulsory school education for their children. Non-governmental organisations with their access to the community should be actively involved in the designing and implementing of such schemes. It is recommended that concessional facilities and loans to employers be extended conditionally upon their not employing child labour. While implementing such schemes, the local community's participation should be sought. Severe penal action should also be taken against those who still persists in employing child labour.[31]

Report on Child Labour in Indian Industries (1981) has observed that though employment of young children is prohibited under various labour enactments, about 40,000 to 50,000 children (below 15 years of age) are working in Sivakasi and the surrounding localities. Enquiries into the cause of such an alarming magnitude of child employment in this particular area revealed some logical and convincing explanations. Sivakashi, situated in Virudhungar district of Tamil Nadu, is a highly drought prone area and thus, the entire rural population suffering from the vagaries of nature and pangs of poverty, is left with no other alternative, but to flock of the local factories of Sivakasi to earn their livelihood. The extreme climatic conditions of the area have a unique influence on the origin and development of the three popular industries of Sivakasi, viz., matchworks, fireworks and printing press, for which the dry climate is a prerequisite. On the one hand, the dry climate and scarcity of rain provide an ideal natural environment for the growth and development of these industries. While on the other, the overall poverty and economic backwardness of the drought-stricken rural population provide abundance of cheap, local labour.[86]

Musafir Singh, V.D. Karura and S.A. Khan in their studies observed that, no enlightened person would deny that child labour is and should be deemed a social problem in the normative context of a modern society. Child labour deprives the child of his education and thereby baulks the development of his potentialities. However, the problem is not degrading and disgraceful in the sense beggary and prostitution are. It is rooted in genuine economic difficulties and must be viewed with sympathy and patience. There is nothing shocking or alarming about the problem when perceived from the perspectives of those who are its unfortunate bearers. In a society where resource distribution is highly skewed, a sizable section of its population is condemned to utilize child labour as a survival mechanism. A significant proportion of the children of the urban poor are participants in the labour force and they cannot be dispensed with through a legislative fiat, however outrageous their presence might be to our social sentiments. As long as the level of our economic development is what it is, any thought of total abolishment child labour would be an unrealistic and unrealisable proposition, a pious intent without a relevance to contemporary social pragmatics. In the absence of possible alternatives, a rash abolitionist measure would simply aggravate the misery of the poor. What therefore, seems feasible and desirable is the dissipation of adverse and unhealthy conditions attendant on child labour rather than its total elimination.[33]

Myron Weiner makes a number of observations in the review of the child labour situation in the Bangalore city market in Secunderabad, in the match, glass and pottery industries, among bounded labourer in Andhra Pradesh and in a village near Pune.

Child labour in India is largely preindustrial, precapitalist labour force. In other works, child labour in India is not the product of industrialism and capitalism, but represents the persistence of the traditional role of the child as worker. Child workers in India are largely illiterate. Most have never been to school and those who attended school drop out before completing fourth standard. Since education is not compulsory, even children of primary school age can be seen working in cottage industries. Few children outside agriculture can be said to the apprentices in traditional family skills. The image of the child as an apprentice to a master craftsman is a romantic one, unrelated to reality. Employers and government officials have a notion of children's work involving speed, patience, manual dexterity, suppleness and so forth, which is of benefit to employers since some of these attributes diminish with age. However, their early use does not necessarily enhance the employability of children as they grow older. Also such early initiation into the labour force is no assurance of a higher wage later. The ban on factory employment of children combined with fewer restrictions on child employment in cottage industries is an inducement for employers to subcontract to smaller shops where wages are lower and working conditions are inferior. While parents gain from the employment of their children—or by using the labour of children at home—it remains unclear how much work would be off the family in the children were in school.[34]

B.N. Chattoraj and Rekha Sexena, in their report, show that in the broader context of the environment which renders children vulnerable to social maladjustment, exploitation and victimisation, an effective and comprehensive strategy in this respect is of utmostneed and importance. In this connection, a purposeful linkage between state intervention and the collective initiatives of the people themselves (with the enlightened groups within the community) would assume a key role. A massive preventive strategy supported by legal aid and assistance must be adopted against victimisation. This would require an optimum use of the resources and potentials of all the sectors of the wider social system. In a country like India which is struggling to overcome the problems of poverty, destitution and neglect, juvenile justice is far more inseparable for social justice.[35]

U.C. Sahoo's report shows that the employment of child labour is the outcome of numerous interrelated factors. The fundamental one is the poor economic structure of the families of the child workers and this is one of the vital causes for the participation of children in the urban labour market. In addition to this, the uncertain growth of capitalism and the consequent rapid inflow of ruralities and the relative failure of the democratic institutions in the country have generated child employment on a mass scale. A solution to this problem may be possible if only drastic steps towards such a goal are taken by the action groups or the trade unions. These organisations must fight for the children's rights and their due position in the Indian society. Subjective, though benevolent, intentions and endeavours can hardly solve the problem of child workers. It seems clear that no significant and decisive steps have been taken towards the elimination of the social exploitation of children. Without the united challenge from the working people themselves, perhaps supported by other democratic and progressive forces, it is difficult to bring about improvement even in the working conditions of the child labourers.[36]

U.C. Sahoo states that mechanisation of agriculture instead of declining the employment of tiny workers, has in fact made them more vulnerable to economic and social exploitation. While capitalism has profitably used the cheap child labour from the exploited social classes and status groups, the continuance of small holdings too necessitated the utilisation of children in the farming. The future of these underaged workforce has been rendered bleak. Intervention of democratic institutions and processes may perhaps ease the situation, but as such the future seems to hold no promise. Obviously, neither the employers nor the States can take any decisive step on their own towards the elimination of this awful exploitation without the united voice of protest from the working people at large, and other democratic and progressive forces. Subjective, benevolent intentions and endeavours can hardly resolve the issue according to Sahoo and he stresses this point in much the same way as he does in his report on child labour in the Surat Textile industry.[37]

R. Vidyasagar's study has provided statistics on the demographic aspects of children (estimated for 1991 based on 1981 population census), health status of children, district-wise infant—and child-mortality rates, nutrition status, health facilities, status of primary education—availability of schools, enrolments and drop-outs—status of child labour (district-wise figures based on 1981 census) and description of the children working in match and fireworks in Tamil Nadu.[38]

Yamuna gives the findings in her study that parental compulsion and economic needs are the predominant reasons for the children joining the work force. Female children earn less than male children. Sex per cent of the working children are subjected to physical punishment at the factory. The reasons put forth by the child workers for not attending school are economic problems, disapproval by parents, and their own disinterest and failure in school examinations. It is found out that 73 per cent of working girls and 39 per cent of boys has never made any effort to find out more about schooling. The parents attach less value for education. The thesis advances some recommendations as to create an awareness among the parents, to offer educational intervention legal measures to eliminate child labour and to introduce changes necessary to make educational system more attractive for the children and their parents.[39]

The Reports of the Royal Commission on Labour (1929-'31) are the earliest attempts to highlight the miserable working conditions of the beedi workers. Consequently, the working of the beedi factories came into focus because of the following reports which brought to light the miserable and inhuman conditions under which the workers toiled while rolling beedis. The Royal Commission observes:

> Many of these places [where beedis are prepared] are small airless boxes, often without any windows, where the workers are crowded so thickly on the ground that there is barely room to squeeze between them. The places are dark semi-basements with damp mud-floor, unsuited for manufacturing process, particularly in industry where workers squat on the floor throughout the working day. Sanitary convenience and adequate arrangements for removal of refuses are generally absent.

Furthermore, the Royal Commission pointed out that while beedi making was carried out in workshops in the bigger cities and towns, it was undertaken as a household vocation in the villages.[40]

The same view was endorsed by the Labour Investigation Committee which was constituted to enquire into the conditions of labour in all industries including beedi, cigar and cigarette industries.[41]

Narayanasamy made an intensive survey of beedi workers in Tamil Nadu. He observed that home workers were predominant in Mukkudal area of Tirunelveli where beedi-making was their main and only occupation. He found prevalence of widespread unemployment among home workers throughout the year except for the peak period of production. He also noted that the workers recruited from other places were employed only at the time of labour scarcity. The survey revealed that the working conditions of the beedi workers were extremely unsatisfactory. Spending the prime of their lives in such miserable environments, workers in general and children in particular appear dismal with yellowish eyes and hollow cheeks.[42]

In the post-independent India, the first survey of the beedi industry was conducted in 1965-66 by the Labour Bureau, Government of India. This survey did not cover workers under home system of work and its scope was restricted to establishments registered under the Factories Act, 1948. The report stated that 79 per cent of the factories numbering 1,338, were located in Andhra Pradesh, Madhya Pradesh and Maharashtra. Some of the major findings of this report are:

1. 49 per cent of the total number of workers were in the beedi factories;
2. The beedi industry employed about 64,400 workers; of whom 95 per cent were production related workers;
3. Only 22 per cent of the production related workers were permanent;
4. The average daily earnings of all workers was Rs. 2.30;
5. Only 2 per cent of the workers were covered under some form of social security benefits such as Provident Fund scheme; and
6. About 40 per cent of the workers were members of some unions.[43]

The report of the National Commission on Labour (1969) identified beedi/cigar industry as a segment of the unorganised sector employing a major portion of the workers. The report further mentions that the organisation of beediworks is monopolised by the contractors who pay wages to the workers on piexe-rate basis. While wages on piece-rate basis itself is an exploitation, the report reveals that there are even deductions made from the wages if the beedis prepared by a worker are of substandard variety or if a worker has wasted some tobacco.[44]

On the recommendations of the National Commission on Labour, the Labour Bureau, once again undertook a survey in 1979 on the working and living conditions of the workers engaged in beedi industry. It was restricted to 20 beedi manufacturing centers spread out all over India. Also this survey which was confined to selected factories within the municipal limits of these centers had a sample of only 1,134 workers including a small number of the home workers. The survey made no attempt to focus on the status of the home workers vis-à-vis the factory beedi workers.

As shown by this survey, the average family income of beedi workers was Rs. 209 per month. At many centers, the various social security measures were not fully implemented by the employers. For instance, only 20.37 per cent of the workers, were covered under the Payment of Gratuity Act, 1972 and this did not include even a single home worker. Only 17 per cent of women workers were getting maternity benefits and this included just 8 per cent of home workers and 9 per cent of shed-workers.[45]

Neerja Chawdhury, in her survey on beedi workers in Madhya Pradesh, found out that of the 54 lakh beedi workers, a large number of them faced conditions of near starvation. There was not enough work for them. Many were, therefore, ready to work for a wage rate lower than the minimum wage rate. The workers were paid a mere Rs. 4, in rural areas, Rs. 4.75 in semi-urban areas and Rs. 5.50 in an urban area for 1,000 beedis rolled by them.[46]

Purushottham's study (1983) presented a profile of 30 beedi workers' households from a village of Chittor district in Andhra Pradesh. The working conditions were characterised by poor earnings, precarious dependence on the job, little awareness about alternative income sources and grinding poverty. This study focused mostly on the plight of male beedi workers.[47]

Mehta made a study on women beedi workers in Vellore, to gauge their awareness about various problems. He found out that practically everyone in the family, from a five year old child to the oldest member of the family, worked for the making and processing of beedis. The practice continued for more than 15 to 20 years without any break. Results drawn from the assessment of the working conditions of the beedi workers revealed that the workers normally got work for three days in a week. The workers got work depending on the supply of raw material. Women beedi workers employed children for folding leaves for which they were paid Rs. 2 per day. The workers were not enjoying the benefits of any of the welfare schemes.[48]

Hussain conducted a study on the exploitation of women and child labour in beedi industry in Samserganj. According to him, women and child labourers were most widespread in the beedi industry where the children were seen at work both at home and workshop. These children worked as helpers to adult workers and their earnings supplemented the family income. The conditions of work were deplorably bad. The children worked in dark, dingy places for long hours resulting in bad health and low productivity.

He also found that women workers constituted 60 per cent of the labour force in the beedi industry and they carried the work mostly at home. They cut and cleaned the leaves for rolling the beedis and worked for long hours without any leisure. Since they did not get any kind of nutritious food, their health was as bad as that of the child labourers. The incidence of T.B. was high among them and many of them also suffered from diseases such as anaemia and ostomalecia. The miserable working condition of the poor women and children has affected the income and health of every family.[49]

A study of child labour some villages of Ayyapuram and Lalkudiyiruppu villages of Tenkasi taluk in Tirunelveli District unfolds that a majority of the women engage themselves in beedi or agricultural work after attending to their household duties. School-going female children and male children assist in this work. Thus, there would be atleast one member in each family doing full time work in beedi making. Besides, the female members earn between Rs. 750 and Rs. 900 per month from beedi rolling which is higher than that of the male members who are employed in agriculture and are earning between Rs. 300 and Rs. 400 per month. The study also reveals that beedi making adds to the income of the household considerably. The researcher finds that the beedi making industry is outside the scope of the Factories Act.[50]

In his study on child labour in beedi rolling in Melapalayam in Tirunelveli, Karunanithi observes that a large number of female workers are engaged in beedi rolling. Out of 112 respondents, 92 respondents (82.4 per cent) are female children. Thousands of children are exploited for economic reasons by their parents who put them to work. The children earn atleast Rs. 5 per day. The children are compelled to work for 10-12 hours per day to complete more or less 500 beedis. Children working within the premises of the beedi companies are exploited by their contractors and employers.[51]

According to the study undertaken by Sheriff, children labour is common in four unorganised sectors: beedi industry, motor garages, garment export companies and domestic services in Chennai and Vellore Town in Tamil Nadu. The study has a sample of 80 child labourers (40 males and 40 females) in the age group of 6-14 years. Out of the

40 males, 20 are beedi workers working in beedi factories in Vellore, and the remaining are employed in other services in Chennai city. This study observes that 85 per cent of the child labourers are living in huts with a monthly family income of more than Rs. 500. All the children working in the beedi factories are drop-outs from school just because their parents could not afford to spend on their education.

Further, the study discloses that children are assigned the task of closing the ends of the beedis or putting the thread around them (84 per cent) and assisting in packing the rolled beedis (43 per cent). It is stated that 55 per cent of beedi workers had fixed hours of work while the rest had no fixed hours of work. Ciild labourers in beedi factories seem to be dissatisfied with their work and feel that their job is strenuous. The study concludes that the children employed in unorganised sectors are neither legally protected by the Minimum Wages Act nor do they have the right to form their own trade union to represent their grievances and demands.[52]

Indian Council of Child Welfare, Tamil Nadu, celebrated a government-sponsored 'Child Labour Day' in Chennai in which workers belonging to various districts of Tamil Nadu participated. The Children Labour Day revealed some startling facts and figures. A first standard child in Vellore rolls 2,000 beedis per day for a meager wage of Rs. 12 an adult worker, for the same amount of work, gets a wage of Rs. 50 per day. There exists thus, a gaping disparity in the wage structure for the same quality and type of work between the child and adult workers. It also brought to light the persistence of bonded labour in this industry in Vellore, despite the government's efforts to eradicate it.[53]

Sharma examines the extent of employment of children, their nature of work and various legislative measures concerning child labour in the country. The author has made some suggestions for their welfare in industries. They are minimum age fixation, medical examination, factory inspector's responsibilities, launching of programmes for the organised sector for the welfare of the child like the trade uinions and a well-channelised contributions of voluntary organisations for their welfare, legislative control and emphasis on educational and vocational guidance.[54]

Mohsin in his paper "Poverty: Breeding Ground for Child Labour" has described the historical development of child labour and the legislative facilities now available for child labour. He has made a sample survey of 43 children belonging to different slum areas of Patna. Ther ages range between 4 to 14 years. Again, acute poverty was found to be the main reason forcing children to seek jobs. Obviously, poverty is the breeding ground for child labour. The investigator suggests a two-side approach to the problem. On the one hand, household poverty should be eliminated and on the other, education should be made compulsory for all children. While the former can be brought about through improved employment and wages and better conditions of work for the householders, the latter can be achieved through incentives in the form of free books, food, clothes and medicines to all school-going children.[55]

Smolowe studies the harmful conditions of child labour in various countries in Asia and in the Pecific, such as, Bangkok, Mexico, South America, the Caribbean, Africa, Central America, Egypt, India and Pakistan. He has tried to analyse the working conditions, legal aspects and socio-economic aspects related to child labour in these countries. Innovative work programmes, such as those adopted in Brazil, are recommended herein, though the researcher seems to be fully aware of the major setback to such a solution in the form of limited resources.[56]

Murthy and Rani attempt to examine the pattern of wages meted out to child labour in small restaurants in the light of the minimum wages prescribed by the State Government. They also probe into the socio-economic variables that motivate the employers to use child labour and the child labourers to get into service. Child labour is characterised by low wages, uncertainty of employment, shifting of employers and jobs and lack of trade unions. It is an example of an unorganised informal sector of the labour market. The wages are fixed on the basis of work load, nature of work, capacity of the employer to pay, strength of the bargaining power of the employee and the hours of work. Apart from this, the wages of child labour have been influenced by various other factors, such as traditions, ethical considerations, levels of income, productivity, production and government policies. The paper examines the impact of such factors on wage determination.[57]

G.P. Mishra and P.N. Pande in their study conducted on child labour in the carpet industry of Mirzapur have reported that child labour is not a simple issue. The existence of child labour is a complex reality, inextricably linked with poverty and under-development. All the same, it cannot be neglected just because the larger and more general problems of poverty and illiteracy are more intractable. Workable solutions ought to be devised to phase out child labour. They aver that the problem, of child labour continues unabated in India largely because of the gap between the policies and legislations on one hand, and the implementation of legislation on the other. And such gap may continue in future also, if a clear-cut policy direction and efforts to prevent children from entering the labour market are not made. The children must enjoy education as a fundamental right and it should be the constitutional duty of the State to realize this right. Therefore to prevent the parents from sending their children to work, the State should protect the parents economically.[58]

G. Karunanithi's study entitled, "Child Labour in North Arcot Ambedkar District: An in-depth study of pledged children in beediworks", covers the production relations, impact of various legal interventions on child labour including the pledge, exploitation and health problems of these children. He points out that the attempts at eliminating child labour have not been successful inspite of several legislative measures. According to the Government of India, the possible solution is to regulate the working condition of children. The duration of work has to be fixed. The health problem of children varies from mild cough to acute tuberculosis. He suggests that compulsory education is an essential measure at present to tackle the problem of child labour. The government and the voluntary agencies have to organize medical camps to identify the specific health problems of children engaged in beediworks. The primary health centers should be strengthened with the installation of adequate infrastructural facilities.[59]

K.K. Khatu, A.K. Tamang and C.R. Rao give a few, specific recommendations based upon the "All India Survey on Working Children" conducted by operations Research Group. Laborious tasks for child labourers should be prohibited. Along with age-restriction for the recruitment of child, there has to be a restriction on the work duration, viz., not more than 3 hours per day. Under the pretext of household work, no child should be deprived of his/her legitimate rights and freedom to do things of his choice under parental care. The main stress is on an enhanced family welfare so that the necessary child care can be attained. It also emphasis dignity of labour, avoiding risky jobs that involve illegal deals and improving the work-environment for child labour.[68]

Soosham Maniar has described the areas of occupational stress among the children of labour force in Ankodia village in Baroda. The exploitation of child labour is a social problem as it has immense adverse effects on the childs in terms of physical, psychological, economical and social growth. A child during his developing years needs security, warmth, love and adequate opportunities for mastering both his physical and social environment. Child labour hampers such a development, exposing the child to undue stress and strain. The stressful situation can arise both from an overload beyond the capabilities of the child and from an underload in which and individual's capabilities are in excess of the demands imposed. A number of legislations and executive orders have been passed from time to time to prevent the employment of children. Despite the existence of many legislative provisions, it is found that our society still inheres the abuse of child labour.[61]

Surjyanarayan Tripathy's study, "Socio-Economic Problems of Child Labour in a Tribal District of Orissa", reveals that child labour is the by-product of poverty coupled with a lack of social awareness. The community must be made to realize the shocking implications and the attendant evils of child labour. This, apparently, cannot be achieved through legislative measures alone. A change in our social attitude will have to be created besides activising the enforcement machinery. Public opinion should be mobilised in addition to a call for the co-operation of voluntary organisations, trade unions and social welfare departments. The study highlights the fact that child labour is prevalent extensively in the lower socio-economic groups not only due to economic compulsions but also because of the lack of an appreciation of their own living conditions. The strategy to eliminate child labour should attack poverty and under-development which form the root cause of child labour. All steps should be taken to increase the family income of the child labourers so that children would not have to work and make both ends meet. Basic education and vocational training should be imparted to the children.[62]

G.P. Mishra and P.N. Pande undertook a study on Child Labour in Glass industry, Ferozabad. It exposes the strong tie that exists between the household and the factory forms of production in the glass industry at system level, and thus reveals the socio-economic system of production and distribution which perpetuates child labour. As a results, the children work for wages and their parents do not send them to school. This also causes abuse of child labour leading to adverse effects on the physical development and health of the working children. The labour laws and other legislature-cum-administrative measures are also ineffective in curbing the use and abuse of child labour in the glass industry. Therefore, some clear-cut policies and efforts are required to prevent the children from entering the labour force; for, a child is a part of a nation's human resource development and human capital. If a policy is drawn to abolish child labour, the State will have to make primary education compulsory. Public awareness of ongoing child welfare schemes should be enhanced for an effective upliftment of these children. Formal education along with vocational training should be introduced and made compulsory.[63]

The studies discussed above are related, in one way or the other, to the present study. However, the present study differs from these studies in several respects. It has certain special features which have been discussed in the succeeding section.

The present study gives primary importance to the levels of exploitation of working children by parents and contractors. An attempt has been made to find out the contribution of the child workers to their family income every month.

The study also attempts to find the extent to which the income of the family is increased due to the employment of children. Further an attempt has been made to study whether the parents from economically backward families force their children to work. Besides analyzing the working and living conditions of the child workers, a special focus has been maintained on the impact of legal intervention in child labour.

Though some of the reports reviewed above have, on a general level, a considerable similarity, this study attempts to survey a wider area of child labour in the beedi industry and aims at a greater comprehensiveness. Such a survey necessitates a suitable methodology for implementation in the beedi industry. For an understanding of the methodology thus employed the introductory chapter of this book can be referred.

REFERENCES

1. S. Kusum, "Poverty—Main Cause of Children Employment", *Lok Kalyan* 2 (January 1990): 16.
2. T.N. Kitchlu, *A Study of Child Labour in Unorganised Industries (A project report*. Delhi School of Social Work, Delhi University, 1986), pp. 31-54.
3. M.S. Krishna Kumari, *Child Labour in Bangalore City* (Delhi: P.S.P.C.K., 1985), pp. 5-9.
4. D.A. Naidu, "Micro Determinants of Child Labour: An Evidence form Rural South India", in D.A. Naidu, Usha Kabadia and Kamini, eds., *Children Labour and Health Problems and Perspects* (Bombay: Tata Institute of Social Sciences, 1986), pp. 74-88.
5. S. Savithiri, "A Survey of Child Labour in Tamil Nadu", in Naidu, Kabadia and Kamini, eds. *Child Labour and Health Problems and Prospects,* pp. 41-64.
6. Khandekar and Mandakini, *A Report on the Situation of Children and Youth in Greater Bombay* (Bombay: Tata Institute of Social Science, 1970), pp. 6-11.
7. *Study of the Working Children in Urban Delhi:* A Report, (New Delhi: Indian Council of Child Welfare, 1997), pp. 11-19.
8. R.N. Pati and S.N. Swain, "Child Labour in Bhubaneswar city", in R.N. Pati, ed. *Rehabilitation of Child Labourers in India* (New Delhi: Ashish Publishing House, 1991), pp. 77-90.
9. Nath Pratima and P.P.K. Majumdar, *Working Children in Calcutta* in Pati, eds., *Rehabilation of Child Labourers,* pp. 165-170.
10. A. Mir, *Child Labour with Special Reference to Carpet Industry of Kashmir: A Socio-Legal Study* (Unpublished Ph.D. Thesis, Kashmir University Library, Srinagar, 1991), pp. 223-261.
11. N.A. Shah, *A Study of Child Labour in Unorganised Sector in Kashmir* (Unpublished Ph. D. Thesis, Kashmir University Library, Sringar, 1991), pp. 11-213.

12. A.N. Singh, *Child Labour in India: Socio-Economic perspective* (Delhi: Shipra Publication, 1990), p. 170.

13. *Report of the National Commission on Labour* (New Delhi: Ministry of Labour, Employment and Rehabilitation, 1969), p. 386.

14. Parveen Nangia, *Child Labour, Cause-Effect Syndrome* (New Delhi: Janak Publishers, 1987), p. 11.

15. Parveen Nangia, *Child Labour,* p. 12.

16. *Report of the National Commission on Labour, 1969* cited by Parveen Nangia, *Child Labour,* p. 12.

17. *Harban Singh Committee Report on the Problems of Child Labour in Various Factories and Industries in Ramanathapuram District,* cited by Parveen Nangia, *Child Labour,* pp. 12-13.

18. *Report of the Committee on Child Labour, 1979* cited by Parveen Nangia, *Child Labour,* pp. 14-15.

19. *Report on the Child Labour in Indian Industries, 1981* cited by Parveen Nangia, *Child Labour,* pp. 15-16.

20. Ramesh Kanbargi, *Child Labour in the Indian Sub-Continent dimensions and Implications,* (New Delhi: Sage Publications, 1991), p. 176.

21. B. Chakravarthy, *Education and Child Labour* (Allahabad: Chaugh Publicaitons, 1989), p. 232.

22. Ivy George, *Child Labour and Child Work* (New Delhi: Ashish Publishing House, 1990), p. 239.

23. A.F. Ferguson & Co. *Child Labour in Fire Cracker Industry—Survey of Middle Income Consumers in Madras City:* A Project Report, cited by R. Vidyasagar, *A Status Report on Child Labour in Tamil Nadu,* (Madras: United Nations Children Education Fund, 1995), pp. 23-24.

24. D. Jayaraj, *Labour Force Participation of Women and Children in Rural Tamil Nadu: An analysis of the inter-district variability* (working Paper No. 3, Madras Institute of Development Studies, Madras, 1993), p. 31.

25. G. Karunanithi, *Assessment of the Status of Primary Education in selected blocks of Kamarajar and V.O.C. Districts of Tamil Nadu* (United Nations Children Education Fund, New Delhi, 1993), pp. 92-100.

26. Madras Institute of Development Studies, *The Match Industry in Saivaksi, Sattur: Towards Removal of Child Labour* (Report submitted to the Ministry of Labour, Government of India, 1985) cited by Vidyasagar, *A Status Report on Child Labour,* pp. 29-30.

27. *Sub-Committee Report on Elimination of Child Labour in the Match and Fireworks Industries in Tamil Nadu,* A Report jointly prepared by representatives of the Department of Labour Employment, Social Welfare and Education in collaboration with United Nations Children Education Fund, 1993, cited by Vidyasagar, *A Status Report on Child Labour,* p. 38.

28. *Report of the Committee Constituted by the Supreme Court of India* (New Delhi: Supreme Court of India, 1991) cited by Vidyasagar, *A Status Report on Child Labour,* pp. 35-36.

29. M. Sumangala and E.S. Nagaarjan, *Economics of Child Labour and Fertility: Study of Peninsular India* (Delhi: B.R. Publishing Corporation (P) Ltd., 1993), pp. 63-85.

30. Helen R. Sekar, G.J. Pinto *Situation of Working Children in Tamil Nadu* (Workshop Report, Child Labour Cell, National Labour Institute, Noida, 1992), p. 60.

31. Mahaveer Jain, *Child Labour in the Gem Polishing Industry in Jaipur* (Noida: Child Labour Cell, National Labour Institute, 1991), pp. 23-31.

32. Manjari Dingwaney with Sunil Dogra, R. Vidya Sagar and Renu Gupta, *Children of Darkness—A Manual on Child Labour in India,* 1988 p. 65.

33. Mussafir Singh, V.D. Kaura, S.A. Khan, *Working Children in Bombay—A study,* (New Delhi: National Institute of Public Co-operation and Child Development, 1978), p. 268.

34. Myron Weiner. *The Child and the State in India* (Delhi: Oxford University Press, 1991), p. 33.

35. B.N. Chattoraj and Rekha Sexena, "Victimisation of Children: An urgent need for effective measures", *Social Change* 20 (September 1993): 23.

36. U.C. Sahoo, "Child Labour in Surat Textile Industry", *Social Change* 20 (September 1993): 36-37.

37. U.C. Sahoo, "Agrarian Dynamics and Child Labour", *Mainstream* 22 (September, 1989): 25-26.

38. R.Vidya Sagar, "Setructural Adjustment Policy and the Child In India", *Status of child in Tamil Nadu* Mardas: M.S. Swaminathan Research Foundation, 1992), pp. 11-30.

39. Yamuna, *Intelligence of child labour attending school and exploratory attempt at educational enter to child workers* (unpublished Ph.D. Thesis, Bharathiyar University, Coimbatore, 1989), p. 203.

40. *Report of the Royal Commission on Labour* (Government of India, 1929), p. 96.

41. *Labour Investigation Committee* (Main Report, Government of India, 1994), p. 46.

42. B.V. Naryanasamy, Report of the Court of Enquiry into Labour conditions in Beedi, Cigar, Snuff, Tobacco—Curing and Tanning Industries (Government of India, 1946, pp. 40-45.

43. *Report of the Committee on Labour Welfare* (Ministry of Labour, Government of India, 1969), pp. 59-70.

44. *Report of the National Commission on Labour* (Government of India, 1969), pp. 477-428.

45. *Report of the Survey and Living Conditions of Beedi Workers* (Ministry of Labour, Government of India, 1978), pp. 169-174.

46. Neerja, Chawdhury, "Beedi Makers in Madhya Pradesh", *Hindustan Weekly* 31 (August 1980): 3.

47. P. Purushottam, "A Profile of Beedi Woekers", *Social Change* 24 (September 1983): 18-23.

48. Prayag Mehta, "Mortagage Child Labour of Vellore Women Beedi Workers' Tale of Woe", *Mainstream* 22 (January 1993): 15.

49. Asfak Hussain, "Exploitation of Women and Child Labour in Beedi Industry in Samserganj", *Social Welfare* 34 (January 1987): 9.

50. S. Pitchaimuthu, "*Child Labour in Beedi Making Industries*", Peninsular Economist (Tiruchirapalli, Association of Economists, 1987-88), p. 79.

51. *G. Karunanithi, "Child Labour in Melapalayam", Social Welfare* 35 (August 1990): 10-11.

52. *Sushila Srivastava and H. Sheriff, "Child Labour in Madras and Vellore",* Social Welfare 38 (September 1991): 14-17.

53. "Plight of Mortgaged Children", *Indian Express,* May 10, 1993, p.3.

54. A.M. Sharma, "Child Labour in Indian Industries". *Indian Journal of Social Work* 40 (March 1979): 345-352.

55. Nadeen Mohsin, "Poverty—Breeding Ground of Child Labour", *Mainstream* 18 (February 1980) 27-29.

56. J. Smolowe, "The Grim Facts about Child Labour". *Readers' Digest* October 1984, pp. 33-41.

57. G.K. Murthy and T.L. Rani, "Wages of Child Labour" *Yojana* 27 (March 1983): 12-14.

58. G.P. Mishra and P.N. Pande, *A Study on Child Labour in Carpet Industyr, Mirzapur* (A Project Report submitted to the Planning Commission, New Delhi, 1992), pp. 158-160.

59. Karunanithi, *Child Labour in North Arcot Ambedkar District: An In-depth Study of Pledged Children in Beediworks* (Project Report submitted to Indian Council of Social Science Research, 1993), pp. 156-171.

60. K.K. Khatu, A.K. Tamang and C.R. Rao, *Working Children in India* (All India Child Labour Survey, Operations Research Group, Baroda, 1993). Pp. 184-186.

61. Sooshma Maniar, *Areas of Occupational Stress among Children in Labour Force in Ankodia Village, Baroda District, Gujarat* (A Project Report submitted to Indian Council of Social Science Research, New Delhi, 1988), p. 78.

62. Surjyanarayan Tripathy, *Social-Economic Problems of Child Labour in a Tribal District of Orissa* (A Project Report submitted to Indian Council of Social Science Research, New Delhi, 1989), pp. 137-138.

63. G.P. Mishra and P.N. Pande, *A Study on Child Labour in Glass Industry, Ferozabad* (A Report submitted to the Indian Council of Social Science Research, New Delhi, 1992), pp. 171-172.

3

Socio-Demographic Profile of Working Children

The present study has been undertaken with a view to find out the variation among the child workers with respect to the variables such as sex, age religion education, household size; income, rural/urban background, process of beediworks, years of experience and place of works. The total samples of 500 child workers taken for this study consist of, 360 (72 per cent) rural child workers and 140 (28 per cent) urban child workers. The rural child workers comprise of 14 boys and 346 girls and urban child workers consist of 16 boys and 124 girls It is hoped that an analysis of these variables would lead to a greater insights.

Table 3.1: Respondents by sex and background

Sl. No	*Sex*	*No of respondents*		
		Rural	*Urban*	*Total*
1.	Boys	14 (3.89)	16 (11.42)	30 (6.00)
2.	Girls	346 (96.11)	124 88.58)	470 (94.00)
	Total	360 (100)	140 (100)	500 (100)

It is clear from the above Table 3.1 that out of the total work force of children, 94 per cent of girls are engaged in

Respondents by Sex and Background

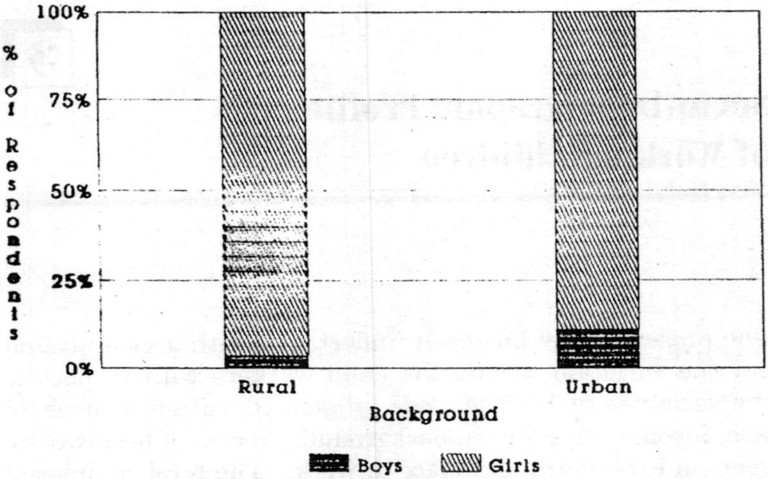

Figure 3.1

beedi making, whereas only 6 per cent of boys do so. Of the total number of rural child workers, 96.11 per cent of girls and 3.89 per cent of boys are engaged in beedi making Among the total urban child workers, 88.58 per cent of girls and 11.42 per cent of boys do the same work Thus, among the rural as well as urban child workers, there are more girls than working boys. And the proportion of working girls is fifteen times as much as the proportion of working boys Thus, the sex discrimination seems to be very much pronounced in this work most of the parents do not compel their boys to take up this work even if they are not interested in studies. They seem to be least bothered about training their sons to acquire the skill in the work in order to make them full-fledged beedi workers in future. They want their boys to secure other better jobs than the beediworks. For instance, a mother in the Melapalayam town has summarized her domestic situation as follows:

> My three daughters are full-time beedi workers. Their present earnings will help them in various wavs at the

time of their wedding and also help to supplement the family income. Therefore, education is not necessary for the betterment of their life. Their present requirement is to acquire the skill of the work in order to promote their life after marriage. This itself is an essential qualification for them to get married. So she can earn for her future. Most of the women in our town have been doing this work since 1945.

But, I do not insist that my ten years old son does this work. I want him to continue his studies up to college level normally, in our town, men rarely engage themselves in this work. They go around and do different types of work. I want my son to have a good career in life. For that, I will educate him by taking loan from various sources.

AGE

The age wise proportions of the child workers seem to vary considerably. It is identified that about half of the workers are in the age group, 12-14;over one-fourth of them are in the age group, 10-12 years; about one sixth of them are in the age group, 8-10 years; but, less than one-tenth of them are in the age group of 6-8 years. This is exhibited in the Table 3.2.

It is evident from the table 3.2 that among the total working children, 49 per cent are in the age group of 12-14 years; 27.60 per cent are in the age group of 10-12 years; 15.80 per cent are in the age group of 8-10 years and 7.60 per cent are in the age group of 6-8 years. Out of the total rural child work force, 49.16 per cent are in the age group of 12-14 years; 30.28 per cent are in the age group of 10-12 years; 14.17 per cent are in the age group of 8-10 years and 6.39 per cent are in the age group of 6-8 years. On the other hand, in the total urban child work force, 48.58 per cent are in the age group of 12-14 years; 20.71per cent are in the age group of 10-12 years; 20per cent are in the age group of 8-10 years and 10.71 per cent are in the age group of 6-8 years. It is found out that the

Table 3.2: Respondents by Age and Background

Sl. No.	Age (in years)	No of respondents		
		Rural	Urban	Total
1.	6-8	23 (6.39)	15 (10.71)	38 (7.60)
2.	8-10	51 (14.17)	28 (20.00)	79 (15.80)
3.	10-12	109 (30.28)	29 (20.71)	138 (27.60)
4.	12-14	177 (49.16)	68 (48.58)	245 (49.00)
	Total	360 (100)	140 (100)	500 (100)

Average (mean) age of rural child work force:11.40 years.

Average (mean) age of urban child work force:11.14 years.

Relationship between background of the child workers and age ($x^2 = 8.16$ df = 3 $p < 0.05$).

average age of child workers from the rural areas is 11.4 years, and from the urban areas is 11.14 years.

It is also found out that the urban children take to the beediworks at the average age of 11.14 years while their rural counterparts do so at the age of 11.4 years. It is thus evident that there is no significant difference between the average age of rural and urban children at which they start working. This has been proved by statistical analysis. However, this shows that the parents do not provide them with primary schooling even. Instead ,they put their children to work and earn money to supplement their family income. Their earnings support their family in several ways.

RELIGION

A majority of Hindu child workers are engaged in the beediworks in the area surveyed except for the Melapalayam town. In the Melapalayam town, the percentage of Muslim child workers is 98. The Christian child workers constitute a very meagre percentage and are in Keelapavoor and Pappakudi blocks. On the whole, a great majority of the child workers are Hindus in the rural areas surveyed whereas in the urban areas, the Muslim child workers are the largest in number. This is figured in the following table:

Table 3.3: Respondents by Religion and Background

Sl. No.	*Religion*	*No of respondents*		
		Rural	*Urban*	*Total*
1.	Hindu	324 (90.00)	23 (16.43)	347 (69.40)
2.	Muslim	12 (3.33)	116 (82.86)	128 (25.60)
3.	Christian	24 (6.67)	1 (0.71)	25 (5.00)
	Total	360 (100)	140 (100)	500 (100)

Respondents by Religion and Background

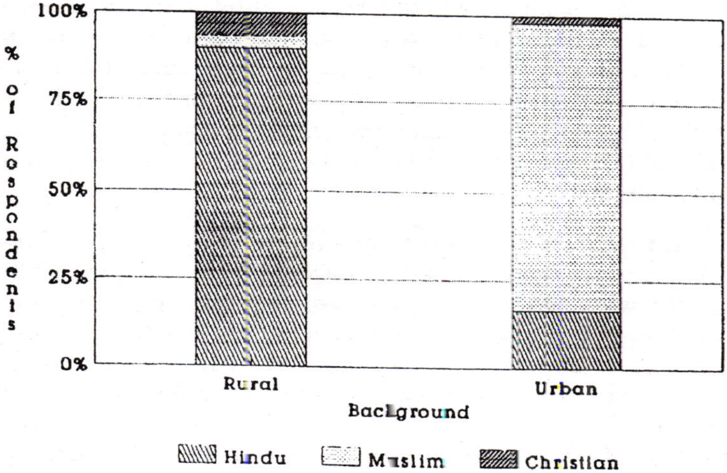

Figure 3.2

The data in table 3.3 clearly show that, among the total child work force, 69.40 per cent are Hindus, 25.60 per cent are Muslims and 5 per cent are Christians. Out of the total rural child workers, 90 per cent are Hindus, 6.67 per cent are Christians and 3.33 are Muslims. Of the urban child workers, 16.43 per cent are Hindus, 0.71 per cent are Christians and 82.86 per cent are Muslim.

Most of the Muslim in the district have settled in urban areas. It is found out that a large majority of Muslims happen to be the natives of various towns in the district. And a considerable proportion of them are found to be full time beedi workers. Of them, a large number of the economically backward Muslim population is engaged in the beediworks. Normally they prefer to work in home-based Industries. It has been a traditional practice among the Muslim community that their women confine themselves to their houses and adhere to the 'Purdha' rules. Therefore, they find beedi making a convenient job. As the work can be carried out at home, many have readily opted for it No doubt, thousands of Muslims women and girl children engaged in this work are the bread winners. They contribute the largest share to their family income.

On the other hand, the Hindu child workers seem to have been initiated into work at a much later stage and are on a part-time or full-time basis. In their early childhood, they engaged in agriculture and other works. Due to the failure of monsoon and unemployment of their parents, the Hindu children enter the beediworks and supplement their family income.

In Christian families, only a limited number of children do the beediworks because the parents send them to schools and also want them to pursue their education up to college level. Their children are encouraged by the local church pastors and religious preachers to study. Almost every village has a school managed by the Christian community. In addition, many foreign Christian Missionaries have established institutions and homes or hostels for poor children. Thus in this district, most of the Christian children are encouraged by these agencies to get education.

Table 3.4: Respondents by Educational Standard, Background and Sex

Sl. No.	Literacy level	No. of respondents							
		Rural			Urban			Grand Total	
		Boys	Girls	Total	Boys	Girls	Total	Boys	Girls
1.	Illiterate	1 (7.14)	42 (12.14)	43 (11.94)	2 (12.50)	21 (16.94)	23 (16.43)	3 (10.00)	63 (13.41)
2.	Primary (I to V std)	6 (42.85)	225 (65.03)	231 (64.17)	9 (56.25)	84 (67.74)	93 (66.43)	15 (50.00)	309 (65.74)
3.	Middle (VI to VIII Std.)	7 (50.00)	79 (22.83)	86 (23.89)	5 (31.25)	19 (15.32)	24 (17.14)	12 (40.00)	98 (20.85)
	Total	14 (100)	346 (100)	360 (100)	16 (100)	124 (100)	140 (100)	30 (100)	470 (100)

Relationship between background of the child workers and their level of education (x^2 –3.68 df = 2 P > 0.05).

Relationship between sex of the child workers and their level of education (X^2 = 6.03 df = 2 P < 0.05).

EDUCATION

The literates among the child workers outnumber the illiterates. A majority of the child workers from the areas surveyed have studied up to primary level. The data exhibit that about one-fifth of the child workers are illiterates, one-tenth of them have studied up to middle school and a limited number of them have studied up to high school. The educational status of the children varies according to their rural/urban background and sex. The table 3.4 illustrates this:

Respondents by Educational Standard and Background

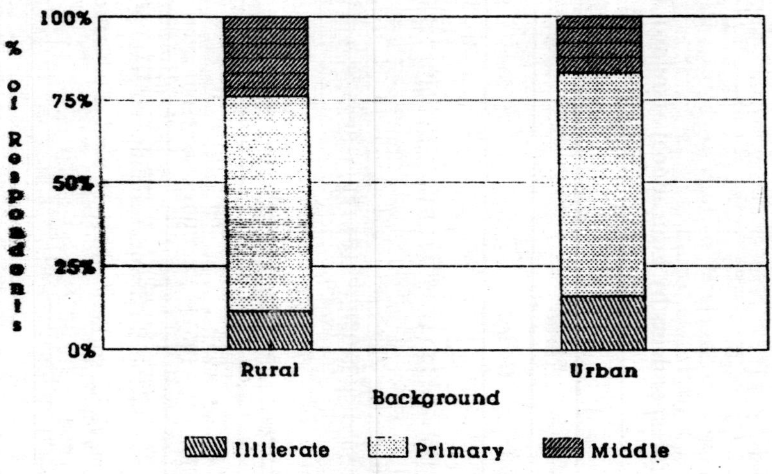

Figure 3.3

It is clear from table 3.4 that in the rural areas 11.94 per cent of the child workers are illiterate, 64.17 per cent have studied up to primary school and 23.89 per cent have received education at middle school level. Of the rural boys, 7.14 per cent are illiterate, 42.85 per cent have studied up to primary school and 50 per cent have continued their studies up to the middle school level. Of the total number

Respondents by Educational Standard and Background

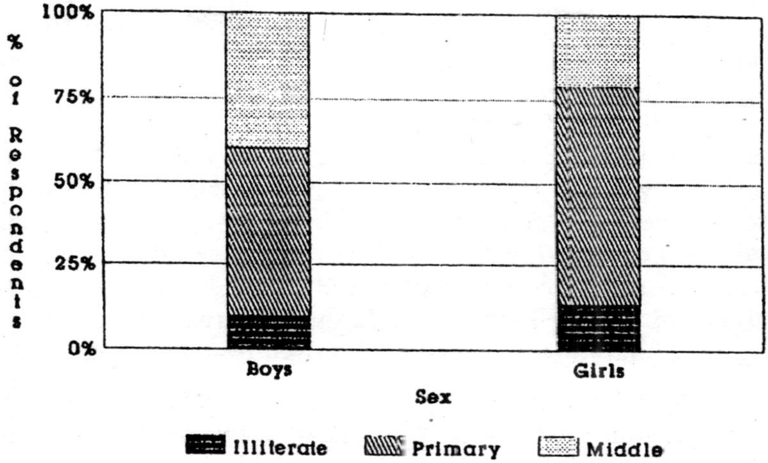

Figure 3.4

of rural girls, 12.14 per cent are illiterate, 65.03 per cent have been educated up to primary school and 22.83 per cent have pursued their studies up to middle school level.

On the other hand, in the urban area, 16.43 per cent are illiterate, 66.43 per cent of them have studied up to primary school and 17.14 per cent have studied up to middle school level. Out of the total number of urban boys, 12.50 per cent are illiterate, 56.25 per cent have studied up to primary school and 31.25 per cent have taken up education up to middle school level. Among the urban girls, 16.94 per cent illiterate, 67.74 per cent have studied up to primary school and 15.32 per cent have had their education so up to middle school.

The analysis of data reveals that the proportion of illiterate child workers in the urban area is more than the proportion of their rural counterparts. In a similar way, the proportion of rural child workers who have studied up to primary school is more than twice the proportion of their urban counterparts. Nevertheless, the proportion of urban child workers who have studied up to primary level, is more than the proportion of their rural counterparts. But, the statistical analysis shows that there is no significant difference between the rural and urban children with respect to their level of education. This analysis of data has resulted in a finding that more urban than rural parents put their children to work after completing primary education. It is also a revelation that more girls than boys have studied up to primary level. But, at middle school level, more boys than girls are educated. From this, one can understand that more than the girls, the boys continue their studies upto a higher standard. But, a majority of the girls pursue their studies up to primary level. It has been proved by a statistical test.

- Generally, the rural areas surveyed are not provided with adequate educational facilities. However, nearly two-thirds of the child workers have studied up to the primary school level. Though a majority of households in these areas are engaged in beedi making, the concentration of this work is not as high as it is in the Melepalayam town. Besides beedi making, there are other sources of income for the rural households, like agriculture, weaving, petty business, etc. Most of the rural families do not depend solely on beedi making for their livelihood. This may be the reason for some of the rural parent allowing their children to study up to middle school level.

Melapalayam is highly concentrated with the beedi making industries. And a great majority (90 per cent) of the people in this town are engaged in this work. Of them, 95 per cent of the workers are Muslims. It is found out that almost all the Muslim households have been doing the work for about half a century. Since beedi making is the only source of income for most of the families, the parents compel their children into beediworks at a tender age. So, they are not able to study up to middle school level. For instance, one of the girls explains her inability to pursue studies as follows:

> I am at present 14 years old. On an average, I work for about 10 hours a day including lunch break. I am doing

the beediworks for the past six years. I have to do the work sitting for hours together with my legs folded I have two brothers and four sisters in my family. I am the eldest child. My father is an unemployed and lazy man. My mother is a sick person. Due to poverty, I have to roll 1,000 beedis per day to supplement my family income. I have studied up to third standard. But, I am very much interested in studies. Unfortunately, my parents prevented me from going to school. Now, I want to study atleast in the night school. Would you help me, sir, to continue my studies? If you do so, I will never forget you in my life time.

HOUSEHOLD SIZE

The small size households are found to be more in the urban areas than in the rural areas. The distribution of households according to their size is shown in the table 3.5.

Table 3.5: Respondents by Household Size

Sl. No.	*Household size*	*No. of respondents*		
		Rural	*Urban*	*Total*
1.	Small (2-4)	48 (13.33)	18 (12.86)	66 (13.20)
2.	Medium (5-7)	247 (68.61)	93 (66.43)	340 (68.00)
3.	Large (8-10)	65 (18.06)	29 (20.71)	94 (18.80)
	Total	360 (100)	140 (100)	500 (100)

Average (Mean) size of households in rural areas = 6.14

Average (Mean) size of households in urban areas = 6.23

Relationship between background of the child workers and their household size ($X^2 = 0.49$ df = 1 $P > 0.05$)

The table 3.5 discloses the data that generally the households surveyed are characterized by medium size (5-7).

It is found that there is no significant difference between rural and urban background of the workers with regard to their household size. In other words, the proportions, of rural and urban households, are more or less similar in all the three categories of the size chosen.

In Tenkasi town, households are small in size. But, in the Melapalayam town, it is relatively large. This may be partially explained in terms of the greater proportion of Muslim population that exists in the town. This community in particular is known for its high fertility rate. Since there is a potential scope for child labour in the town, the children from the Muslim households are engaged in the beediworks from on early age. Especially, the parents rely more on their daughters than their sons with respect to this work. The Melapalayam town, more crowded than the villages, was surveyed for the present study. The town is invariably busy from 8 a.m. to 10 p.m. with beedi making. One can see the heaps of wasted beedi leaves in various places within the town. The houses are littered with the waste leaves and tobacco dust.

EARNINGS OF CHILD WORKERS

The efficiency of the child workers depends upon the total number of beedis they make per day. Their efficiency is determined by their places of residence, sex, and especially by their background. The categorization of child workers on the basis of the total number of beedis they produce per day is given in table 3.6.

The work efficiency of child workers can be explained in terms of the total number of beedis they make per day. It is found out that the proportion of rural children who make less than 500 beedis per day is relatively more than the proportion of their urban counterparts. But, the proportion of urban children who make 500-1,000 beedis per day is relatively more than the proportion of their rural counterparts. Thus, it is evident that the efficiency of the urban children is relatively more than that of the rural

Table 3.6: Respondents by Total Number of Beedis Made Per Day, Background and Sex

Sl. No.	Number of beedis made per day	No. of respondents							
		Rural			Urban			Grand Total	
		Boys	Girls	Total	Boys	Girls	Total	Boys	Girls
1.	Less than 500 beedis	7 (50.00)	263 (76.01)	270 (75.00)	6 (37.50)	83 (66.94)	89 (63.57)	13 (43.33)	346 (73.62)
2.	500 to 1,000 beedis	7 (50.00)	83 (23.99)	90 (25.00)	10 (62.50)	41 (33.06)	51 (36.43)	17 (56.67)	124 (26.38)
	Total	14 (100)	346 (100)	360 (100)	16 (100)	124 (100)	140 (100)	30 (100)	470 (100)

Relationship between background of the child workers and number of beedis made per day (X^2 = 6.50 df = 1 P > 0.05)

Relationship between Sex of the child workers and number of beedis made per day (X^2 = 12.78 df = 1 P < 0.05)

Respondents by Number of Beedis Made Per Day and Background

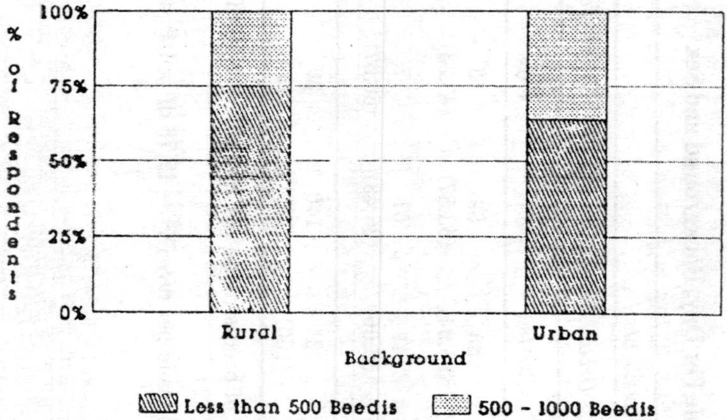

Figure 3.5

Respondents by Number of Beedis Made Per Day and Sex

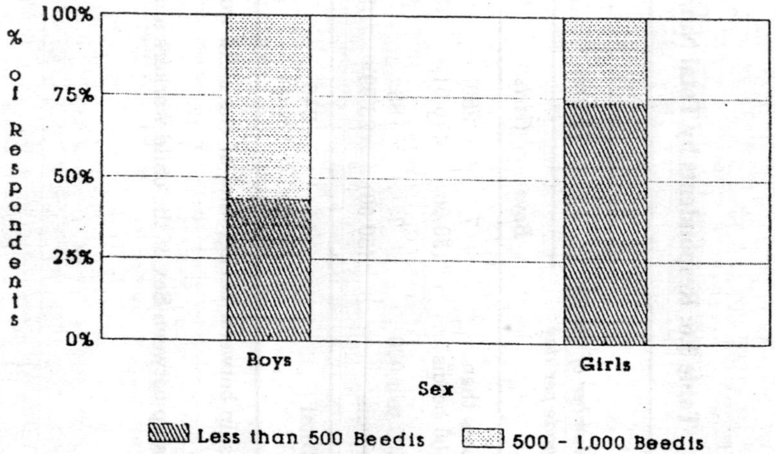

Figure 3.6

children. It is, therefore, concluded that background of the children has a decisive role to play in determining their efficiency. It has been supported by the result of a statistical test.

In a similar way, there is a relationship between the sex of the children and their work efficiency. The data in the Table 3.6 shows that the proportion of boys who make 500-1,000 beedis per day, is more than twice the proportion of the girls who make that range of beedis. This clearly shows that the boys are more efficient than girls with regard to making beedis. This has been proved by a statistical test.

It has already been observed that the parents force their children to complete the prescribed quota of beedis per day. Both rural and urban children undergo this pressure to reach a target of 1,000 beedis per day. Girls, especially are often subjected to this pressure that they will produce her prescribed quota for the day.

One possible reason for this trend is that while the rural children are not so much pressurized by their parents, the urban parents pressurize their children. In the case of the latter, if they do not complete the target of a day, they are punished cruelly. Hence, if they fall short of their target, the children borrow beedis from professional lenders. For the borrowed beedis they have to pay an interest, of one beedi for every ten beedis per day. But, after sometime, they find it very difficult to return the beedis along with the interest. This practice of *Vatti Beedi System* is in existence in blocks such as Keelapavoor, Alangulam, Pappakudi, Kadayam and Tenkasi. In course of time, this would amount to disastrous consequences. For instance, a 14 year old girl from Keelapavoor used to borrow beedis from a beedi lender whenever there was a shortage of beedis to complete a day's quota. Her debt with interest gradually increased to several hundred beedis. After some months, she realised that she would not be able to repay the debt of beedis with interest. She became depressed as she was afraid of her parents.

Gripped by fear she committed suicide by jumping into a well.

The average monthly income of the child workers has been calculated from the total number of beedis they make per month excluding usual holidays. It is presented in the table 3.7.

The data show that 18.89 per cent of rural child workers earn up to Rs. 200, 69.1 per cent of them earn Rs. 200-400 and 11.94 per cent of them earn Rs. 401-600. Of the total number of rural boys, 28.57 per cent of them earn up to Rs. 200, 57.14 per cent of them earn Rs. 200-400 and 14.29 per cent of them earn Rs. 401-600. Out of the total number of rural girls, 11.85 per cent of them earn up to Rs. 200, 69.65 per cent of them earn Rs. 200-400 and 18.50 per cent of them earn 401-600.

In the urban area, 20 per cent of the child workers earn upto Rs. 200, 53.57 per cent of them earn Rs. 200-400 and 26.43 per cent of them earn Rs. 401-600. Of the total number of urban boys, 43.75 per cent of them earn up to Rs. 200, 50 per cent of them earn Rs. 200-400 and 6.25 per cent of them earn Rs. 401-600. Out of the total number of urban girls, 16.94 per cent of them earn up to Rs. 200, 54.03 per cent of them earn Rs. 200-400 and 29.03 per cent of them earn Rs. 401-600.

It is clear from the analysis that those who earn less than Rs. 200 are un-skilled workers, those who earn Rs. 200-400 are semi-skilled workers and those who earn Rs. 401-600 are skilled workers. Both in rural and urban areas, a majority of the child workers are semi-skilled workers. There are more skilled workers in the urban areas than in the rural areas. Therefore, the earnings of the urban children is generally higher than that of their rural counterparts. It has been proved by a statistical test.

In one way or the other, the parents are dependent on their children for their income to maintain their family.

Table 3.7: Respondents by Monthly Income, Background and Sex

Sl. No.	Monthly Income (Rs.)	No. of respondents							
		Rural			Urban			Grand Total	
		Boys	Girls	Total	Boys	Girls	Total	Boys	Girls
1.	Upto Rs. 200	4 (28.57)	41 (11.85)	68 (18.89)	7 (43.75)	21 (16.94)	28 (20.00)	11 (36.67)	62 (13.19)
2.	Rs . 200-400	8 (57.14)	241 (69.65)	249 (69.17)	8 (50.00)	67 (54.03)	75 (53.57)	16 (53.33)	308 (65.53)
3.	Rs . 401-600	2 (14.29)	64 (18.50)	43 (11.94)	1 (6.25)	36 (29.03)	37 (26.43)	3 (10.00)	100 (21.28)
	Total	14 (100)	346 (100)	360 (100)	16 (100)	124 (100)	140 (100)	30 (100)	470 (100)

Average (Mean) monthly income of rural child workers = Rs. 286.11

Average (Mean) monthly income of urban child workers = Rs. 312.86

Average (Mean) monthly income of boys in total = Rs. 246.72

Average (Mean) monthly income of girls in total = Rs. 316.27

Relationship between background of the child workers and their monthly income ($X^2 = 17.07$ df = 2 $P < 0.05$)

Relationship between Sex of the child workers and their monthly income ($X^2 = 10.00$ df = 2 $P < 0.05$)

Respondents by Monthly Income and Background

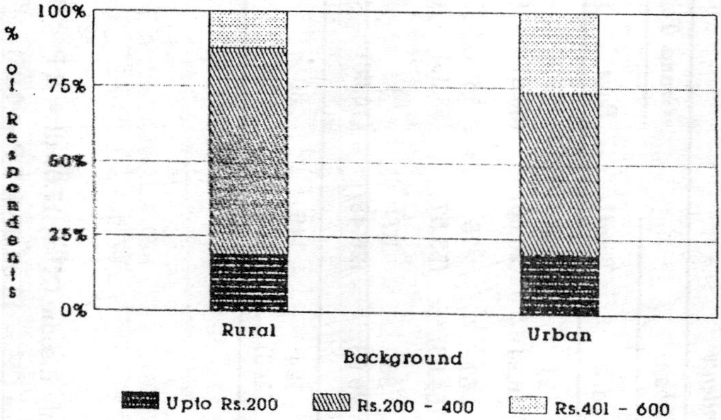

Figure 3.7

Respondents by Monthly Income and Sex

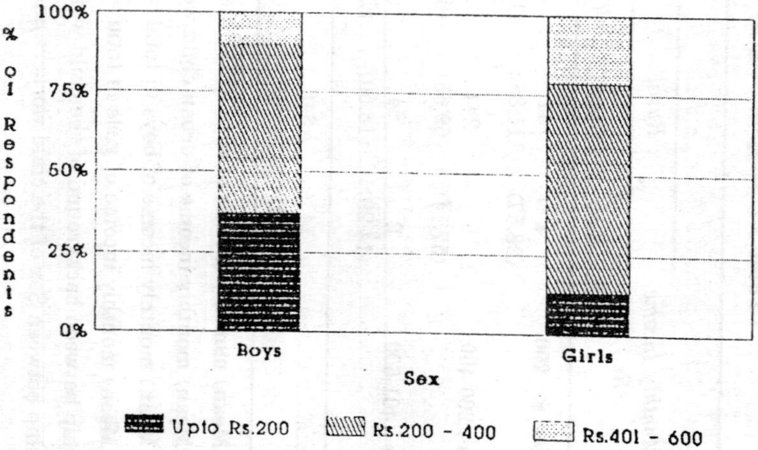

Figure 3.8

Thus, the overall contribution by the child workers to the total monthly income of their households is rather significant. Hence, from the parents point of view, the contribution of more than one skilled child worker would make a considerable increase in the family income.

The analysis of data discloses that the earning of boys is more than the earning of girls. For instance, the boys who earn Rs. 401-600 per month, are more than twice the number of girls who earn a similar income. This shows that there is a significant relationship between the children s sex and their earning capacity. This has been supported by a statistical test. It is, therefore, concluded that the earning capacity of girls is more than the earning capacity of boys.

However, it has already been proved that the work efficiency of the boys is more than that of girls in the areas surveyed for the study. When the regularity of children in their work is considered, the girls are more regular and systematic in their work than boys. The reason is that the parents compel their girl children to confine themselves to the beediworks. They prescribe the number of beedis per day for their girl children according to their skill and compel them to complete this daily quota. This practice has gradually increased their production capacity and made them full-fledged workers in course of time. But, the boys are not trained in this manner. There is no compulsion on their part to stick on to the target as their parents want them to take up some other wok than beedi making. This is the reason why the earnings of the boys are less than that of the girls.

It is important to mention that almost all the child workers from rural areas are basically home-based. They work with their family members. Most of them do not know the details about the total number of beedis they make per day and the emoluments for making so many beedis in a day. Their parents collect money from the contractors or owners who supply raw material periodically. Sometimes, the parents send their children to receive the money from the contractors or owners. But, they are not to spend a portion of their earnings to buy the things which they desire. Some of them would press their parents for some money to buy some eatables and small articles from the nearby petty shops. For instance, a girl of 12 years in Nalankurichi village in Alangulam block, explains her plight as follows:

> I have been in the beediworks since I was seven. I have studied up to II standard. For the last six years, I have been toiling without relief. Initially, I was trained by my mother. Gradually, I picked up this work. At present, I make 750-1,000 beedis per day. On an average, I earn Rs 21 per day. Sometimes, my mother would visit the beedi company to give the finished beedis and get the money; some times I do so. Once I took Rs. 4 from my wage to buy glass bangles from a local pettyshop. For that, I was severely scolded and beaten up by my parents. My father is a drunkard and an irresponsible person. Though I am a potential earning member in my family, I do not have any liberty to spend money from my wage to buy certain articles for my use.

One cannot ignore the fact that for a majority of the families the working children provide a substantial contribution to the total income. In a family with a single son or daughter, it is absolutely possible for the parents to manage the household economy without extracting work from their child. In case of a large family with more children, employment opportunity should be given to the parents so that the children could be educated and be relieved from this drudgery.

HOUSEHOLD INCOME

A majority of the households fall under the income category of Rs. 501-1,000. Less than 10 per cent of households come under the income category of below Rs. 500. The classification of rural and urban households according to their monthly income, is shown in the table 3.8.

Table 3.8: Household by Income and Background

Sl. No.	Household size	No. of respondents		
		Rural	*Urban*	*Total*
1.	Upto 500	39 (10.83)	7 (5.00)	46 (9.20)
2.	501-1,000	178 (49.44)	51 (36.43)	229 (45.80)
3.	1,000-1,500	80 (22.23)	46 (32.86)	126 (25.20)
4.	Above 1,500	63 (17.50)	36 (25.71)	99 (19.80)
	Total	360 (100)	140 (100)	500 (100)

Average (Mean) monthly income of households in rural areas = Rs. 897.07

Average (Mean) monthly income of households in urban area = Rs. 1,892.30

Relationship between the background of the child workers and their family income ($X^2 = 15.40$ df $= 3$ $P < 0.05$)

The proportion of rural households in the income category of Rs. 501-1,000 is relatively higher than the proportion of their urban households in the same income category. On the other hand, the proportion of urban households in the income category of Rs. 1,001-1,500 is relatively higher than the proportion of the rural households. It has been worked out that the average monthly income of rural households is Rs. 897.07, whereas it is Rs. 1,892.30 for urban households. It is, therefore, concluded that the monthly income of urban households is more than the monthly income of the rural households. This is supported by a statistical test.

The reason for this wide difference in income between rural and urban households is explained in terms of the greater employment opportunities available in the urban area surveyed. For example, getting jobs in tea-stalls, hotels, provisional stores and other shops are possible in the urban area.

Since agriculture is a seasonal work, the income of the rural households is rather low and unsteady. As a result of this, a majority of the rural households earn (monthly) up to Rs. 1,000 through beedi making. But, in the urban areas, majority of the households earn Rs. 1,000 and above. This is so in the town because the household members do not really solely on beedi making.

PROCESS OF BEEDIWORKS

The process of beedi making includes cutting the tendu leaves, beedi rolling, closing the beedi ends and bundling the beedis. It is clear from the analysis of the survey data that in rural areas a majority of the children are engaged in all the different stages in beedi making. But in the urban areas, a majority of the children are engaged in beedi rolling and closing the beedi ends. This is presented in table 3.9.

It can be seen from the table 3.9 that out of the total number of child workers, a majority of the urban child workers do more than one type of work. On the other hand, a majority of the rural child workers do all types of work rather than their urban counterparts. It is reported that more rural than urban workers are trained n such a way to pick-up all types of work in beedi making within 2-3 years. The acquiring of skill in the work depends on the experience and background of the children. That is, there is a significant relationship between the background of the children and the types of work they do. It is inferred from this that the proportion of rural children who do al types of work is higher than the proportion of urban children who are skilled similarly. This has been proved by a statistical test.

The rural children are entrusted with the responsibility of all sorts of work relating to beedi making such as moisturing and cutting the leaves, rolling beedis, closing the

Table 3.9: Respondents by Type of Beediworks, Background and Sex

Sl. No.	Type of Beediworks	No. of respondents							
		Rural			Urban			Grand Total	
		Boys	Girls	Total	Boys	Girls	Total	Boys	Girls
1.	More than one type of work	5 (35.71)	158 (45.67)	163 (45.28)	9 (56.25)	80 (64.52)	89 (63.57)	14 (46.67)	238 (50.64)
2.	All types of work	9 (64.29)	188 (54.33)	197 (54.72)	7 (43.75)	44 (35.48)	51 (36.43)	16 (53.00)	232 (49.36)
	Total	14 (100)	346 (100)	360 (100)	16 (100)	124 (100)	140 (100)	30 (100)	470 (100)

Relationship between background of the child workers and type of work they do (X^2 = 13.49 df = 1 $p < 0.05$)

Relationship between sex of the child workers and types of work they do (X^2 = 0.18 df = 1 $P < 0.05$)

Respondents by Types of Beediworks and Background

Figure 3.9

beedi tips, typing the beedi mouth with the help of thread and bundling. The parents compel them to make a fixed number of beedis per day. On the other hand, the urban children concentrate on one or two types of work relating to beedi making. The reason is that their parents and other family members share the work with their children. Therefore, the children prefer a particular type of work, especially rolling or closing the ends of beedis. However, they are not compelled by their parents to complete the target in a day.

It is found that the proportion of boys is higher than the proportion of girls with regard to the types of the beediworks they do. In other words, the proportion of boys who do all types of work is higher than the proportion of the girls who are capable of a similar skill. Nevertheless, the difference in their proportion is negiligible. Therefore, it is understood that there is no significant relationship between the sex of the children and the types of work they do. This is supported by a statistical test.

PLACE OF WORK

Child workers make beedis at their homes or the homes of their neighbours and friends The analysis of data reveals that a great majority of the children make beedis at their homes themselves. Other children make beedis in their neighbours' and friends houses. This is presented in table 3.10.

It is evident from table 3.10 that out of the total number of rural child workers, 71.94 per cent of them make beedis at their homes and 28.06 per cent of them do it in their neighbouhood. Of the total number of rural boys, 85.71 per cent of them do the work at their homes and 14.29 per cent of them do it in their neighbourhood. Among the total number of rural girls, 71.39 per cent of them make beedis at their homes and 28.61 per cent of them do it in their neighbourhood.

Table 3.10: Respondents by their Place of Work, Background and Sex

Sl. No.	*Place of work*	*No. of respondents*							
		Rural			*Urban*			*Grand Total*	
		Boys	*Girls*	*Total*	*Boys*	*Girls*	*Total*	*Boys*	*Girls*
1.	Home	12 (85.71)	247 (71.39)	259 (71.94)	14 (87.50)	84 (67.74)	98 (70.00)	26 (86.67)	331 (70.43)
2.	Neighbourhood	2 (14.29)	99 (28.61)	101 (28.06)	2 (12.50)	40 (32.26)	42 (30.00)	4 (13.33)	139 (29.57)
	Total	14 (100)	346 (100)	360 (100)	16 (100)	124 (100)	140 (100)	30 (100)	470 (100)

Of the total number of urban child workers, 70 per cent of them make beedis at their homes and 30 per cent of them do it in their neighbourhood. Out of the total urban boys, 87.50 per cent of them do the work at their homes and 12.50 per cent of them do it in their neighbourhood. Of the total urban girl children, 67.74 per cent of them make beedis at their homes and 32.26 per cent of them do it in their neighbourhood. On the whole, the proportion of girls who do the work in their neighbourhood, is more than twice the number of boys who do so.

It is important to note that, both in rural and urban areas, girls normally work in their neighbourhood. Particularly, more urban girls than their rural counterparts work in their neighbourhood. Such practice is very much noticed in the Malapalayam town. But, it is rarely seen in Keelapavoor and Kadayam blocks. Both in rural and urban areas, a great majority of the boys work at their homes. They do not like to carry out the work in their neighbourhood.

LENGTH OF EXPERIENCE

The service of the child workers in the beediworks has been categoriesd as below 4 years, and above 4 years for the purpose of analysis. It is observed that those with the service of more than 4 years have acquired more skill in this work than those with service of less than 4 years. Therefore, worker with less than 4 years of service make less than 500 beedis per day, whereas those with more than 4 years of service would produce about 1,000 beedis per day. This is exhibited in table 3.11.

It is clear from table 3.11 that the proportion of urban children (64.29 per cent) with above four years of service in the beediworks, is more than the proportion of their rural counterparts (60.56 per cent) with the same years of experience. It seems that there is a connection between the background of the child workers and their years of experience in the beediworks. However, chi-square test has proved that there is no significant relationship between the two variables.

Table 3.11: Years of Service of Respondents in Beediworks, Background and ex

Sl. No.	Service in years	No. of respondents							
		Rural			Urban			Grand Total	
		Boys	Girls	Total	Boys	Girls	Total	Boys	Girls
1.	Below 4 years	9 (64.29)	133 (38.33)	142 (39.44)	11 (68.75)	32 (25.82)	43 (30.71)	20 (66.67)	165 (35.11)
2.	Above 4 years	5 (35.71)	213 (61.50)	218 (60.56)	5 (31.25)	92 (74.18)	97 (69.29)	10 (33.33)	305 (64.89)
	Total	14 (100)	346 (100)	360 (100)	16 (100)	124 (100)	140 (100)	30 (100)	470 (100)

Average (Median) years of service in rural areas = 4.23 }
Average (Median) years of service in urban areas = 4.38 } Based on the classification of years of service as 0-4; 4-6 and 6-8.

Relationship between the background of the child workers and their service in beediworks (X^2 – 3.30 df = 1 P > 0.05)

Relationship between the sex of the child workers and their service in beediworks (X^2 = 12.06 df = 1 P > 0.05)

Respondents by Years of Service and Sex

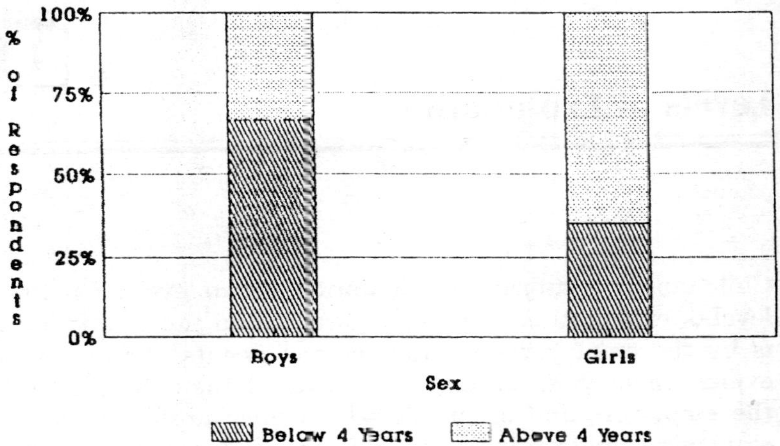

Figure 3.10

However, there seems to be a significant relationship between the sex of the child workers and their years of service in the beediworks. In other words, the proportion of girls (64.89 per cent) with more than four years of service in the beediworks, is nearly twice the proportion of boys (33.33 per cent) with same years of service. Thus, there is a significant relationship between the two variables. It is proved by the statistical test. It is understood from this analysis that the girls start making beedis earlier than the boys. This finding has already been discussed.

4

Levels of Exploitation

Child labour is subject to exploitation at two levels. The first level of exploitation is by their parents and the second level is by the employers, contractors and agents. The parents exploit their children for the survival of their families and the employers and others do so for their profit. However, employing children in various jobs especially at their tender age will uncompromisingly affect their career in future. This chapter attempts to discuss the exploitation of child labour at these levels.

REASONS FOR JOINING BEEDIWORKS

It is generally considered that illiteracy, ignorance, poverty, low wages and unemployment of family members are the major causes of child labour. Madan says: "the children are required to seek employment either to augment the income of their families or to have a gainful occupation in the absence of availability of school going facilities at various places".[1] It is important and necessary that the most crucial causes for child labour are discussed here.

POVERTY

In India, poverty drives the parents to put their children to work. The diseases affecting the family members and other contingencies make them incur debt. Under such circumstances, parents resort to employ their children as they find no other alternative to earn more money. Hence, a large majority of the children are engaged in the beediworks in order to supplement their family income.

The inadequate wages of adult workers necessitate them to compel their children to work for some wage. And, the employer takes advantage of these children by providing work for a pay that is lower than what he would normally pay the adult workers. That is, the entry of the children into employment makes labour cheap. Most employers think that a lot of work can be extracted from the children at the work place and this labour is very cheap in comparison with that of an adult worker. In fact, it ensures them of a wider margin of profit without any additional, new investments. For instance, in India, children are employed as domestic servants because their labour is cheap. Besides, the prevalence of poverty within the workers' family is a stimulus to the employers who desire to secure cheap labour in order to get more profit. Thus, child labour exists because they provide cheap labour and not because they are better workers.

In the area surveyed for the present study, the parents compel their children to take to employment because the family income is very low. Had their income been adequate, they might not have pushed their children to make beedis. The children are made to work because the adult wage-earners in their families are either unemployed or underemployed. The children engaged in the beediworks contribute substantially to their family income.

NON-IMPLEMENTATION OF COMPULSORY EDUCATION

Absence of any provision for compulsory education is an important cause of child labour. If education is made compulsory for the children below fourteen years, the children will attend schools. It is the best way to prevent children from entering the labour market. Mostly children who do not have access to schools at the initial stage, take some jobs as desired by their parents. This was indirectly admitted by the National Commission on Labour, 1969. It has stated in its report that "the gradual reduction in the employment of child labour since Independence is due partly to the expansion of educational facilities by the States and also to relatively better enforcement of statutory provisions relating to child labour".[2]

The parents consider their working children economic assets. Their desire to educate their children becomes a double liability as they incur a loss in their family income on the one hand, and on the other hand, educational qualification by itself does not guarantee employment. Generally, the parents seem to be least the concerned with their children's future. They are satisfied with what they gain by the earnings of their children. Thus, the children are deprived of educational opportunities and vocational training. The gross ignorance on the part of the parents is the cause for not sending their children to school. Addam condemns this as follows:

> The child labourers today will be the paupers of tomorrow. There are boys and girls who will grow up without either formal schooling or knowledge of a trade. Sooner or later, their youthful energies exhausted, they will become dull, shiftless and driftless.[3]

ABSENCE OF SCHEMES FOR FAMILY ALLOWANCES

In India, there are no family allowances for those whose earnings are inadequate to meet their family requirements, while, some sort of an allowance is given in a number of countries like Australia, New Zealand, United Kingdom and France. If such allowances are given, they may not send their children to work. The amount that is being paid to widows as compensation or pension is rather insufficient to maintain their family without the addition of their children's income.

Of all the areas surveyed, Melapalayam is the most popular town for beediworks. A large majority of people in the town have been doing their work for over 60 years. Several beedi companies were established during the post-independence period. After 1950, beedi making became a permanent occupation for a great majority of the households of the town. People who were engaged in weaving abandoned

Table 4.1: Respondents by Reasons for doing Beediworks, Background and Sex

Sl. No.	Reasons	No. of respondents							
		Rural			Urban			Grand Total	
		Boys	Girls	Total	Boys	Girls	Total	Boys	Girls
1.	Compelled by Parents	10 (71.43)	279 (80.64)	289 (80.28)	13 (81.25)	96 (77.42)	109 (77.86)	23 (76.67)	375 (79.79)
2.	Others	4 (28.57)	67 (19.36)	71 (19.72)	3 (18.75)	28 (22.58)	31 (22.14)	7 (23.33)	95 (20.21)
	Total	14 (100)	346 (100)	360 (100)	16 (100)	124 (100)	140 (100)	30 (100)	470 (100)

that occupation after Independence, since export of textile items to Burma, Ceylon and Singapore was stopped. Thus people found the beediworks to be the viable alternative to weaving.

In a similar way, a large majority of households in Pappakudi, Keelapavoor, Kadayam, Alangulam and Tenkasi blocks have also been doing this work since 1960. Initially, the beediworks was introduced in Mukkudal in Pappakudi block. Then it got spread over other blocks in this district. Those who were engaged in agriculture also gradually shifted to the beediworks owing to the failure of monsoon.

It is evident from the table 4.1 that, of the rural child workers, 80.28 per cent of them are compelled by their parents to take up the beediworks. Out of the rural boys, 71.43 per cent are compelled by their parents to do the work. Out of the rural girls, 8.64 per cent of them are compelled by their parents to take up the work. It is, therefore, concluded that a great majority of children, especially the girls, do the work out of the pressure given by their parents.

A similar trend is found among the urban child workers in this regard. The boys-and-girls constitution shows a similar proportion with respect to their employment, which is more often than not a compulsion by their parents.

The other reasons such as time passing, puberty, traditional work, the lack of schools in the neighbourhood and earning money while staying at home, are also represented by a limited number of respondents.

A girl of 13 years, engaged in the beediworks in Sivanunadaroor, in Kadayam block, explains her plight as follows:

> My parents are basically agricultural labourers and absolutely unfamiliar to the beediworks. But, they forced me to work due to severe financial crisis in our family. Though I was promoted to the fifth standard, I

had no other option but to resort to the beediworks. I have three sisters and two brothers. My father is underemployed. My mother is sick. My brothers and sisters are younger than me. So, I have to earn for the survival of my family. There is no other source of income for my family. I have to make thousand beedis per day. I am very much interested in studies. But, the situation warrants me to confine to this work.

I. Exploitation at Parental Level

The exploitation by the parents themselves is common in the areas where child labour is concentrated. This is the first level of exploitation that children experience in their childhood.

ON BEEDI MAKING

The parents compel their children to make beedis even at a tender age of 6 to 7. However, it is important to study the attitude of the children towards the beediworks. Of all the areas surveyed, a great majority of the child workers do not like to do this work, whereas less than one-tenth of them like to do the work. It is exhibited in the table 4.2.

It can be seen from table 4.2 that there is no significant relationship between the background and sex of the children on the one hand and their liking of the beediworks on the other. That is, the background and sex of the child workers do not influence their attitude towards beedi making in a significant way. It is proved by the statistical test.

An attempt was made to know the reasons given by the child workers for not liking the beediworks. A large majority of the children do not like the work because this work has prevented them from pursuing their study. About one-fourth of them do not like the work because it is a painful job. The reasons given by the child workers are presented in table 4.3.

In rural as well as urban areas, a large majority of girls say that they cannot study because of the beediworks. This

Table 4.2: Respondents by their Liking of Beediworks, Background and Sex

Sl. No.	Child workers liking of beediworks	*No. of respondents*							
		Rural			*Urban*			*Grand Total*	
		Boys	*Girls*	*Total*	*Boys*	*Girls*	*Total*	*Boys*	*Girls*
1.	Liking	3 (21.43)	30 (8.67)	33 (9.17)	2 (12.50)	12 (9.67)	14 (10.00)	5 (16.67)	42 (8.94)
2.	Not Liking	11 (78.57)	316 (91.33)	327 (90.83)	14 (87.50)	112 (90.33)	126 (90.00)	25 (83.33)	428 (91.06)
	Total	14 (100)	346 (100)	360 (100)	16 (100)	124 (100)	140 (100)	30 (100)	470 (100)

Relationship between the background of the child workers and their liking of beediworks ($X^2 = 0.09$ df = 1 $P > 0.05$)

Relationship between the sex of the child workers and their liking of beediworks (($X^2 = 1.97$ df = 1 $P > 0.05$)

Table 4.3: Respondents by Reasons for Not Liking Beediworks, Background and Sex

Sl. No.	*Reasons for not liking beediworks*	*No. of respondents*							
		Rural			*Urban*			*Grand Total*	
		Boys	*Girls*	*Total*	*Boys*	*Girls*	*Total*	*Boys*	*Girls*
1.	Prevented from pursuing study	6 (54.55)	209 (66.14)	215 (65.75)	7 (50.00)	64 (57.14)	71 (56.35)	13 (52.00)	273 (63.79)
2.	Painful Work	2 (18.18)	85 (26.89)	87 (26.61)	2 (14.29)	33 (29.46)	35 (27.78)	4 (16.00)	118 (27.57)
3.	Hazardous Work	1 (9.09)	9 (2.85)	10 (3.06)	2 (14.29)	4 (3.57)	6 (4.76)	3 (12.00)	13 (3.04)
4.	Prevented from playing with others	1 (9.09)	8 (2.54)	9 (2.75)	2 (14.29)	6 (5.36)	8 (6.35)	3 (12.00)	14 (3.27)
5.	Under Payment	1 (9.09)	5 (1.58)	6 (1.83)	1 (7.13)	5 (4.47)	6 (4.76)	2 (8.00)	10 (2.33)
	Total	11 (100)	316 (100)	327 (100)	14 (100)	112 (100)	126 (100)	25 (100)	428 (100)

clearly shows that the child workers do the work out of compulsion by their parents. However, more than one-fourth of the rural and urban children do not like the work because it is a tedious one. But, the proportion of the child workers who express reasons other than not liking this work, is negligible.

HOURS OF WORK

During the survey, a number of child workers have reported to be working for more than eight hours per day. The distribution of the child workers according to the number of hours they work is given in table 4.4.

It is clear from table 4.4 that about 30 per cent of rural child workers and 35 per cent of their urban counterparts work for about 8 hours per day. Thus, there is a considerable difference between the background of the child workers and the number of hours they work in a day. This has been proved by a statistical test.

Similarly, about 40 per cent of the boys work for about 8 hours per day, but about 35 per cent of girls only do so. On the other hand, the proportion of girls (about 65 per cent) is higher than the proportion of boys (60 per cent) with respect to the number of hours they work per day. This shows that there is a significant relationship between the sex of the respondents and the number of hours they work. This is proved by a statistical test.

It is observed during the survey that the children continue to work with their parents especially, with their mothers, even after 10 p.m. Sometimes, they have to sit till mid-night with their parents to complete the quota for the day. It is important to note that the children work for long hours under pressure both from their parents and employers. The contractors fix a time to return the beedis completed. If a worker fails to return the beedis within the given time, the contractors refuse to supply the raw material for the next day and, moreover, do not take the completed beedis into

Table 4.4: Respondents by Duration of Work, Background and Sex

Sl. No.	Duration of work	No. of respondents							
		Rural			Urban			Grand Total	
		Boys	Girls	Total	Boys	Girls	Total	Boys	Girls
1.	Upto 4 Hrs.	– (0.58)	2 (0.56)	2 (12.50)	2 (3.23)	4 (4.29)	6 (6.67)	2 (1.28)	6
2.	4-8 Hrs.	4 (28.57)	101 (29.19)	105 (29.17)	6 (37.50)	56 (45.16)	62 (44.29(	10 (33.33)	157 33.40)
3.	Above 8 Hrs. (8-12)	10 (71.43)	243 (70.23)	253 (70.27)	8 (50.00)	64 (51.61)	72 (51.42)	18 (60.00)	307 (65.32)
	Total	14 (100)	346 (100)	360 (100)	16 (100)	124 (100)	140 (100)	30 (100)	470 (100)

Average (Mean) hours of work by rural child work = 8.79

Average (Mean) hours of work by urban child work = 7.89

Average (Mean) hours of work of boys = 8.13

Average (Mean) hours of work by girls = 8.56

Relationship between the background of the child workers and duration of work (X^2 = 15.75 df = 1 $P < 0.05$)

Relationship between the sex of the child workers and duration of work (X^2 = 9.00 df = 1 $P < 0.05$)

Chi square has been worked out by classifying the children according 8 hrs. and above 8 hrs.

account for payment. Therefore the children are under pressure to complete the beedis within the prescribed time. This makes them work for long hours and even late into the night. For instance, a girl reports as follows:

> My parents compel me to sit upto 11 p.m. to complete the prescribed quota for a day. Every morning at 9.30 I have to handover the completed beedis to the beedi company. One day, due to ill-health, I was not able to complete my target within the prescribed time. On that day, I went to the beedi company half an hour late. But, the accountant refused to accept the beedis and also to supply the raw material for the next day. That day we all suffered without food. So, our parents severely scolded and punished me. Sometimes, I had to borrow vatti beedi from a professional lender to avoid this sort of critical situation. And for that, I had to pay one beedi extra for every 10 beedis.

Thus, one can understand from the discussion that the children suffer from physical fatigue and mental stress because of long hours of work. This is perhaps why most of the children do not like this work.

PUNISHMENT

By and large, the child workers are punished by their parents in many ways if they do not complete the given quota for a day. They are punished if they are not sincere in their work. In rural and urban areas, a majority of the children are scolded and beaten by their parents for these reasons. Sometimes, they are not allowed to go out to play and are denied food. The distribution of data relating to this is given in table 4.5.

The data in table 4.5 show that more rural boys than their urban counterparts are punished. Of the rural child workers, more girls than boys are punished. As a great majority of the parents depend upon their children's income, they deny their children food and play in case they do not

Table 4.5: Respondents by Types of Punishments, Background and Sex

Sl. No.	Types of punishment	No. of respondents							
		Rural			Urban			Grand Total	
		Boys	Girls	Total	Boys	Girls	Total	Boys	Girls
1	Scolding only	3 (21.43)	99 (28.01)	102 (28.33)	15 (93.75)	42 (33.87)	57 (40.71)	18 (60.00)	141 (30.00)
2.	Scolding and beating	4 (28.57)	114 (32.95)	118 (32.78)	—	35 (28.23)	35 (25.00)	4 (13.33)	149 (31.70)
3.	Denial of food and not allowed to go out to play	4 (28.57)	105 (30.35)	109 (38.28)	—	41 (33.06)	41 (29.29)	4 (13.33)	146 (31.06)
4.	No punishment	3 (21.43)	28 (8.09)	31 (8.61)	1 (6.25)	6 (4.84)	7 (5.00)	4 (13.34)	34 (7.24)
	Total	14 (100)	346 (100)	360 (100)	16 (100)	124 (100)	140 (100)	30 (100)	470 (100)

Relationship between the sex of the child workers and punishment ($X^2 = 1.50$ df = 1 $P > 0.05$) | Chi-square has been worked out by classifying punishment and no punishment.

complete the prescribed number of beedis for the day. Girls especially, are subject to more humiliation, harassment and sometimes, severe punishment rather than boys. More often than not, it is the girl children who are expected to abide by a set target and are forced with rigour towards the reaching of that target. Instead of allowing their children to enjoy their childhood, the parents exploit them and also punish them heavily. Sometimes, the contractors scold the children for not submitting the completed beedis within the stipulated time and also for not maintaining the quality in making beedis.

INCENTIVES

It is observed that some children are rewarded by their parents depending on their performance of work. About one-fourth of them are rewarded in terms of appreciation. More urban children than their rural counterparts get such appreciation and gifts from their parents. This is shown in table 4.6.

Repondents by Types of Reward and Background

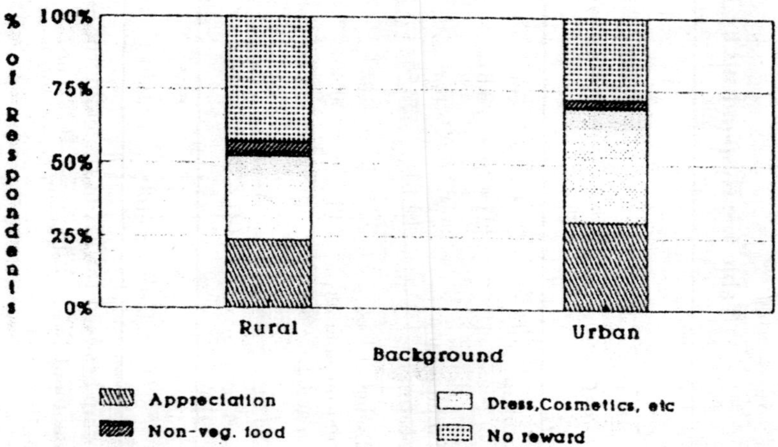

Figure 4.1

Table 4.6: Respondents by Types of Reward, Background and Sex

Sl. No.	Types of reward	No. of respondents							
		Rural			Urban			Grand Total	
		Boys	Girls	Total	Boys	Girls	Total	Boys	Girls
1.	Appreciation	8 (57.14)	77 (22.25)	85 (23.61)	7 (43.75)	36 (29.03)	43 (30.17)	15 (50.00)	113 (24.04)
2.	Providing new set of dress cosmetics, etc.	2 (14.29)	102 (29.48)	104 (28.89)	5 (31.25)	49 (39.52)	54 (38.57)	7 (23.33)	151 (32.13)
3.	Providing non-vegetarian food	-	17 (4.91)	17 (4.72)	-	4 (3.23)	4 (2.86)	-	21 (4.47)
4.	No reward	4 (28.57)	150 (43.36)	154 (42.78)	4 (25.00)	35 (28.22)	39 (27.86)	8 (26.67)	185 (39.36)
	Total	14 (100)	346 (100)	360 (100)	16 (100)	124 (100)	140 (100)	30 (100)	470 (100)

Relationship between the background of the child workers and reward ($X^2 = 9.47$ df = 1 $P < 0.05$)

Relationship between the sex of the child workers and reward ($X^2 = 1.92$ df = 1 $P > 0.05$)

Chi-square has been worked out by classifying reward and no reward for the children

It is clear from the data from table 4.6 that in rural as well as in urban areas none of the boys were provided with non-vegetarian food, whereas in the rural areas, a limited number of girls is treated to this luxury of non-vegetarian. But, more or less a majority of boys are rewarded in terms of appreciation, i.e., parents express their love in terms of words. About one-third of the girls are rewarded with gifts such as bangles, cosmetics and the like. In urban and rural areas, a lesser number of girls than the boys get such gifts. It is understood from this that boys are more encouraged and appreciated by their parents than the girls. It is proved by a statistical test. However, parents are very particular about earning money by employing their children but they do not bother about their children's need for love, or their expectations and suffering. Even when they are sick, they are forced to complete the prescribed quota.

For instance a girl of 13 years reports as follows:

> I have been doing the beediworks for the past six years. Now I make 1,000 beedis per day. It have one sister and three brothers. My sister is also working along with me. My father is an assistant in a local tea shop. He is drawing Rs. 850 per month. But, he gives Rs. 350 to our family. But, our family needs more than this money to fulfil our basic needs. So, my sister and myself have to work in order to supplement our family income. Daily I am forced to make 1,000 beedis. Otherwise, my parents scold me. If I complete my work in advance, they ask me to make more beedis. Sometimes, I make 1,250 beedis a day. There is no encouragement or appreciation from my parents. It is my fate that I undergo this ordeal every day.

It is understood that the incentives given to the child workers are not for their development. But, it is in a way a kind of bait used by the parents in order to extract more work with the intention of earning more money.

GETTING MONEY TO SPEND ON THEIR OWN

Generally, it is reported that the proportion of the children who do not get pocket-money from their parents is more than the proportion of children who get it. Both in rural and urban areas, more than the girls, boys get money to spend on their own. This is presented in table 4.7.

It is evident from table 4.7 that about one-fourth of child workers only, irrespective of their background and sex are given money to spend on their own. However, it is proved by a statistical test that there is no significant relationship between the children who get pocket money on the one hand and their background and sex on the other. Normally, the child-workers spend the money on buying eatables from the local petty shops. The main reason for giving money is to encourage the children into doing more work.

For instance, one of the girls explains her painful experience as a beedi worker, as follows:

> I work for about 10 hours per day. I have to do the work by sitting with folded legs for hours together. Sometimes, I am made to work for more than 10 hours. My parents compel me to work till I complete the target set for a day. Due to my heavy workload, I have lost the chance of playing with my friends from neighbouring houses and other childhood activities. Daily I am earning Rs. 20. But, it would be handed over to my father. I cannot take even single paise from my wages. If I want to get any article or eatable it will be done only through my parents with some limitation. Sometimes, I get a meagre amount as pocket money when I make more beedis than the prescribed number of beedis for a day.

This clearly shows that the practice of the parents giving money to their children is not born out of any deep concern for the welfare of their children, but it is aimed at getting more money by making the children work with renewed vigour.

Table 4.7: Respondents by Getting Pocket Money, Background and Sex

Sl. No.	Getting Pocket Money	No. of respondents							
		Rural			Urban			Grand Total	
		Boys	Girls	Total	Boys	Girls	Total	Boys	Girls
1.	Yes	4 (25.57)	92 (26.59)	96 (26.67)	6 (37.50)	43 (34.68)	49 (35.00)	10 (33.33)	135 (28.72)
2.	No	10 (71.43)	254 (73.41)	264 (73.33)	10 (62.50)	81 (65.32)	91 (65.00)	20 (66.67)	335 (71.28)
	Total	14 (100)	346 (100)	360 (100)	16 (100)	124 (100)	140 (100)	30 (100)	470 (100)

Relationship between the background of the child workers and getting pocket money (X^2 = 3.41 df = 1 P > 0.05)

Relationship between the sex of the child workers and getting pocket money (X^2 = 0.29 df = 1 P > 0.05)

RECREATION AND ENTERTAINMENTS

The children engaged in the beediworks have, in one way or another, lost their childhood which is a period of innocent joy and happiness. The child beedi workers make beedis almost all through the day. They work under constant pressure as they are supposed to complete the target. They are therefore, not able to enjoy their childhood. They do not have any recreation or entertainment such as playing, watching television, seeing films, listening to radio and visiting friends.

Besides making beedis, boys get to play with others more commonly than the girls. The proportion of rural girls who never play is higher than the proportion of their urban counterparts. On the whole, only a very small group of working children play sometimes. But the rest of them have almost given up their play which is one of the most joyous activities of childhood that promotes the physical and mental development of the children.

The mass media such as radio, cinema and television are the main sources of entertainment for the children engaged in the beediworks. However radio is an easily available medium that entertains the poor, rural sections of population at large. This is the reason why the majority of the child beediworkers listen to most of the radio programmes in a day while making beedis. Some of them listen to only select programmes. Boys, more than the girls, listen to the radio programmes and, also, more rural children than their urban counterparts have the habit of listening to radio.

Cinema is the most popular medium that attracts various sections of population including the beedi workers. However, more than three-fourths of the children have no time to see cinema. And here too, more boys than girls see cinema irrespective of their background.

Though television has become easily accessible even to villagers, it still seems to be beyond the reach of the beedi workers. That is perhaps the reason why over one-third of the children watch only selective television programmes. However, they watch television mostly in their neighbours' houses. Nearly two-thirds of the children do not have the chance of watching television in their neighbours' houses since they are engaged in beedi making for the whole day. It is understood that more boys that girls watch the television programmes. Nevertheless, a majority of the rural as well as urban children do not have the chance to watch the television programmes.

Visiting friends and relatives is also a source of entertainment for the child workers. A great majority of the children have no chance of visiting their friends and relatives. More boys than girls visit friends and relatives. It is found that rural children have more chances to visit their friends and relatives than that of their urban counterparts.

Thus, it is clear from this analysis that generally entertainment is restricted considerably due to the work pressure which prevails over the child workers all through the day. They confine themselves to their houses and make beedis for 10-12 hours in a day. Thus, these children sacrifice their childhood activities and shoulder many of the family responsibilities. They have no leisure. It is reported that the young children instead of playing with the children of their age group, toil for the sake of their families. They have been denied the joyous phase of childhood. The child workers are denied education, recreation and play. This can be tackled by the implementation of compulsory primary education. If any child is denied education, play and other types of entertainment at this tender age, they will grow with a sense of discontentment and depression which will remain throughout their lives. Thus, the child beedi-workers are deprived of their right to be care-free as children and their right to education. The burden of work cause various types of health problems, especially bronchitis and tuberculosis. These diseases affect them physically and mentally.

Most parents use their children to assist them in their work and produce more beedis in order to earn more money. But, on the contrary, in the study areas, the children are the potential workers who use of the assistance of their parents for their work. Sometimes, the mother will assist them in bundling work. The target number of beedis to be rolled for the day is fixed for each child. In other words, when the beedi workers are not able to complete their target set for a day, they will be compelled to borrow beedis without their parents' knowledge from the shop owners or private beedi workers or professional lenders with the condition that they should return the beedis with an interest, i.e., one beedi for every 10 beedis for a day. This is called Vatti Beedi System which is very much prevalent in Tirunelveli District. A majority of the beedi workers spend three to four hours a day to make beedis in order to clear off the debt. However, they are not able to overcome this syndrome. Vatti Beedis get multiplied day by day. Ultimately, the girls have no way of repaying the debt of beedis and commit suicide. It is reported that in Alangulam and Keelapavoor blocks, two girls committed suicide for this reason.

ASSISTING IN HOUSEHOLD CHORES

The study discloses that a great majority of the children, besides beedi making, assist their parents in the household chores such as fetching water, cleaning vessels, cooking, shopping and cleaning the house. This is shown in table 4.8.

The data in table 4.8 show that 97.78 per cent of the children workers assist their parents in household work in addition to beedi making, whereas only 2.22 per cent of them are free from such extra work. There is no significant difference between the rural boys and girls in terms of their assistance in this regard. A similar trend is observed to be existing in the case of the urban boys and girls too.

It is evident from the above analysis that a great majority of the children assist their parents in household work irrespective of sex and background. In other words, the parents extract work from their children not only to make

Table 4.8: Respondents by Assisting in Household Work, Background and Sex

Sl. No.	Household Work	No. of respondents							
		Rural			Urban			Grand Total	
		Boys	Girls	Total	Boys	Girls	Total	Boys	Girls
1.	Assisting	13 (92.86)	339 (97.98)	352 (97.98)	16 (100)	115 (92.74)	131 (93.57)	29 (96.67)	454 (96.60)
2.	Not Assisting	1 (7.14)	7 (2.02)	8 (2.22)	-	9 (7.26)	9 (6.43)	1 (3.33)	16 (3.40)
	Total	14 (100)	346 (100)	360 (100)	16 (100)	124 (100)	140 (100)	30 (100)	470 (100)

beedis but also to accomplish their household duties. Thus, the children are doubly exploited by their parents, by engaging them in beedi making and assigning some household chores.

For instance, a girl of 10 years engaged in the beediworks in a village near Kadayam explains her problems as follows:

> I have been doing the beediworks since I was a 6 year old. I have two sisters and one brother. My mother is a beedi worker. Now she is affected by T.B. My father is a farmer. But, in our area, there is no employment opportunity in agriculture. Due to inadequate family income I am engaged in this work. My two elder sisters are also beedi workers. My younger brother is studying in a local primary school. Since my mother is sick, I have to carry out the household work in addition to making 500-700 beedis in a day. I have to clean my house, clean the vessels and assist my mother in the beediworks for 8-9 hours per day to make 500-750 beedis. I wake up at 5.00 a.m. and go to bed at 10.00 p. m. after completing the household work.

DEPRIVED OF EDUCATION

The main cause of illiteracy in rural and urban areas is the inability of the parents to afford education for their children. When compared to the proportion of literature girls, the proportion of illiterate boys is very low. Of the total number of illiterate children, the rural illiterates are twice as much as their urban counterparts. The children provide various reasons for dropping out of schools. Of the total drop outs, three-fourths of them say that their parents are too poor to afford them education and one-tenth of them say that they are not interested in pursuing their studies.

The analysis of data reveals that, both in rural and urban areas, the main reason for dropping out of schools is poverty. Unlike their rural counterparts, the urban girls do not like studies. Lack of interest on the part of the children, poverty and the need to supplement their family income are the reasons expressed by many of the children. The parents want their children to pick-up beedi making within the age of 9-10 years. If so, they will be able to earn some money to meet the family expenditure and a major portion of the expenditure towards their marriage. They also think that the skill in beedi making would help their daughters to continue the work, even after their marriage.

The parents are partial to their daughters with regard to their education. They allow their sons to get education atleast upto high school level, but they restrict the education of their daughters to primary or middle school level. They say that the skill in beedi making is an important qualification for the daughters at the time of their marriage. The girls who are engaged in the beediworks, continue to be beedi workers for life. Thus, they live as beedi workers and die as beedi workers. The parents do not want their sons to be beedi workers. They prefer agriculture or other work for their sons.

Though the children express several reasons for dropping out of school, a majority of (about 90 per cent) them like to attend school irrespective of their age. However, all the sample children say that education would increase employment opportunity and promote economic development. They also feel that education would improve the ability to read and write, and enhance their self confidence, social status and better marriage prospects. It is interesting to find that two-fifths of the total number of children want to study upto high school level and one-fifth of them want to pursue upto higher secondary level. The proportion of rural children who want to study higher secondary or college education is higher than the proportion of their urban counterparts, because in rural areas, at a very early age, the children are forced to take part in the beediworks to earn money. More than the girls, boys are willing to join arts colleges technical schools. Both in rural and urban areas, a majority of the children want to study upto high school level.

During the survey, a girl of 12 years reports as follows:

I have no parents. Now I am residing with my relatives. I had never been to school. I am very much interested in studies. But my aunt (guardian) forced me to do the beediworks. My uncle and aunt are very particular about my earnings. For the last six years, I have been doing this work. I am forced to make 1,000 beedis per day. I have no knowledge of writing and reading. I am earning Rs. 22 per day. But, I am not able to sign in my beedi company accounts book as I am an illiterate. I want to be a literate. But, I am not able to go to school regularly. I am prepared to attend night school to make myself literate.

The discussion in this section presents the plight of children engaged in the beediworks. The focus is on the exploitation of the children by their parents themselves. They are deprived of childhood activities, education, recreation and the like. In short their childhood is lost owing to the irresponsibility of their fathers who want their children to make substantial contribution to their family income. They want their children to shoulder major responsibilities and are shirking their own responsibilities. Therefore, it is in no way an irrelevant claim that the parents themselves are the first level exploiters of their children.

II. Exploitation at Contractor Level

Besides exploitation of children by their parents, they are subject to a second level of exploitation by their contractors. This level of exploitation has been discussed in detail in this section.

SUPPLY OF RAW MATERIAL

The contractors, sub-contractors, agents of beedi companies and private shops supply the raw materials to the household for making beedis. It is collected by the child workers or their parents. It is reported that a large majority of the households get raw material from the contractors and also from beedi companies directly. This is presented in table 4.9.

Table 4.9: Respondents by Supply of Raw Material, Background and Sex

Sl. No.	Supplier of Raw material	No. of respondents							
		Rural			Urban			Grand Total	
		Boys	Girls	Total	Boys	Girls	Total	Boys	Girls
1.	Contractor/owner of Beedi company	14 (100)	332 (95.95)	346 (96.11)	15 (93.75)	121 (97.58)	136 (97.15)	29 (96.67)	453 (96.38)
2.	Neighbours	-	13 (3.77)	13 (3.61)	1 (6.25)	2 (1.61)	3 (2.14)	1 (3.33)	15 (3.19)
3.	Purchase from Market	-	1 (0.28)	1 (0.28)	-	1 (0.71)	1 (0.71)	-	2 (0.43)
	Total	14 (100)	346 (100)	360 (100)	16 (100)	124 (100)	140 (100)	30 (100)	470 (100)

The table 4.9 discloses that, of the total respondents from rural households, 96.4 per cent of them get raw material from their contractors and beedi companies, 3.2 per cent of them get them from their neighbours and 0.4 per cent of them purchase them from the local market. It is found out that there is no significant variation between the rural and urban respondents with respect to getting raw materials.

It is clear from the analysis of the survey data that over 90 per cent of the respondents from rural and urban areas get raw materials from their contractors and beedi companies. Most of the villages and towns have branches of beedi companies. But, a few villages do not have such branches in their area. Therefore, these villagers get raw materials from their neighbours or purchase them from local market. And the beginners to the beedi making profession also get the raw material from their neighbours or purchase them from the local market. The contractors and beedi companies supply raw material mostly to the skilled and experienced workers.

COLLECTION OF RAW MATERIAL

Usually, the raw material is collected by parents, elders and child workers. It is found out that in the areas surveyed, a majority of child workers collect the raw material from the beedi companies and contractors. However, the proportion of rural child workers who collect raw material is nearly twice that of their urban counterparts. This is exhibited in table 4.10.

On the whole, nearly three-fourths of the children collect raw-material. There is a significant difference between the rural and urban children in terms of collecting raw materials. This is proved by chi-square test.

It is found out that most of the beedi companies issue pass-books in the name of women workers. In rural areas, the parents get pass-books in the name of their children by giving a false age. These children have direct dealing with the contractors and collect raw material for themselves. It

Table 4.10: Collection of Raw Material by Household Members and Background

Sl. No.	Collection of raw material	No. of respondents		
		Rural	Urban	Total
1.	Parents and other family members	63 (17.50)	80 (57.14)	143 (28.60)
2.	Child Workers	297 (82.50)	60 (42.86)	357 (71.40)
	Total	360 (100)	140 (100)	500 (100)

Relationship between the background of the child workers and collection of raw material (X^2 = 77.57 df = 1 P < 0.05)

is estimated that over three-fourths of the rural child workers collect raw material directly from the contractors irrespective of the question whether the pass-books are on their names or on the name of their parents. But in the urban areas, there is no such misrepresentation of the child's age in getting pass-books. So, a majority of the pass-books are on their parents name. Normally, the urban parents collect raw material sometimes, they send their children to do so. It is understood from the analysis that the rural child workers outnumber their urban counterparts with regard to the collection of raw material from the contractors.

ADEQUACY OF RAW MATERIAL

Most of the rural as well as urban parents and children report that the raw material supplied is inadequate to make the required number of beedis. Normally, 500 gms., of tendu leaves and 200 gms., of tobacco dust are supplied to them to make 1,000 beedis. If the leaves are in good quality, a skilled worker can make about 850 beedis with the quantity of leaves supplied. In case the leaves are of second-rate or of poor quality, the worker can make a maximum 600 beedis

Collection of Raw Materials by Household Members and Child Workers

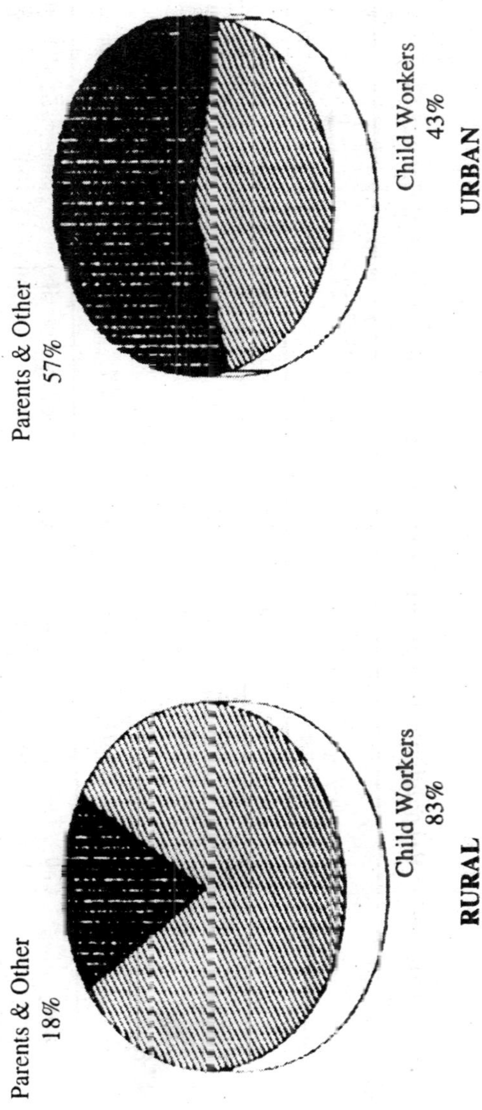

Figure 4.2

Table 4.11: Respondents by their Views on the Adequacy of Raw Material and Sex

Sl. No.	Raw material	No. of respondents								
		Tobacco			*Leaf*			*Thread*		
		Boys	*Girls*	*Total*	*Boys*	*Girls*	*Total*	*Boys*	*Girls*	*Total*
1.	Adequate	1 (3.33)	28 (5.96)	29 (5.80)	2 (6.67)	13 (2.77)	15 (3.00)	22 (73.33)	345 (73.40)	367 (73.40)
2.	Inadequate	29 (96.67)	442 (94.04)	471 (94.20)	28 (93.33)	457 (97.23)	485 (97.00)	8 (26.67)	125 (26.60)	133 (26.60)
	Total	30 (100)	470 (100)	500 (100)	30 (100)	470 (100)	500 (100)	30 (100)	470 (100)	500 (100)

instead of the prescribed target of 1,000 beedis. Therefore, the worker has to purchase extra leaves from outside. Sometimes, the tobacco dust is also poor in quality. It is dampened deliberately to increase its weight. This in turn decreases the quantity of tobacco dust for the beedi maker. Therefore, the beedi workers need to purchase the tobacco dust from outside to reach the target. The supply of poor quality of leaves and tobacco dust is the main reason for this shortage. The respondents' views on the adequacy of raw material are presented in table 4.11.

It is evident from table 4.11 that an overwhelming majority of boys and girls report that the raw materials are inadequate to produce the prescribed number of beedis. However, nearly three-fourths of them say that the thread provided to tie the mouth part of the beedi, is adequate.

The analysis shows that over 90 per cent of the respondents get inadequate raw material, i.e., they are not able to make the prescribed number of beedis out of the raw material supplied to them. The inadequacy of leaves and

Adequacy of Raw Material and Sex

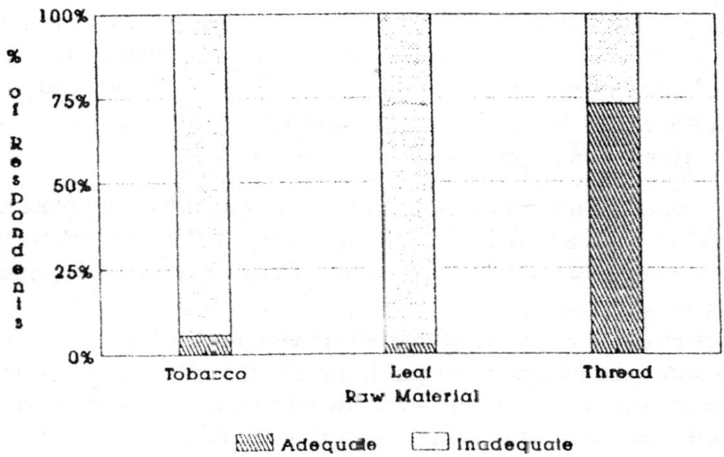

Figure 4.3

tobacco is mainly due to the manipulation of the contractors at the time of weighing them. The moistened tobacco dust supplied to the beedi workers weighs 200 gms., exactly at the tie of supply. But, afterwards, there is a considerable shortage of the tobacco dust when it gets dried. Even if the beedi leaves are weighed correctly, most of them are not of good quality. Some are shorter, rough and damaged. All these contribute to the inconsistency between the supply of raw material and prescribed number of beedis to be made. In addition to this, some contractors and agents demand atleast 100 beedis as Commission Beedis for every 1,000 beedis. This is in fact an extra burden to the children.

SHORTAGE OF RAW MATERIAL

The shortage of raw material is adjusted by purchasing them from the local market. A majority of the households spend Rs. 9-10 to purchase raw materials to make 1,000 beedis. Some households spend Rs. 13 and above to do so. This is supported by the figures distributed in table 4.12.

The average expenditure incurred by the rural and urban children has been worked out at Rs. 9.6 and Rs. 9.5 respectively. The expenditure on raw material incurred by the rural as well as urban child workers, is more or less equal. Therefore, there is no significant relationship between the background of the children on the one hand and the amount spent by them for the purchase of extra material on the other. It is supported by a statistical test.

But, the average amount of money spent by the boys and girls has been worked out to be Rs. 8.9 and Rs. 9.7 respectively. Thus, the girls spend a little higher than what the boys spend on the shortage of raw materials. In addition to this, the proportion of girls (34.68 per cent) who spend Rs. 11 – 14 on the shortage of raw material is nearly thrice as much as the proportion of the boys who do so. There is therefore, a significant relationship between the sex of the children and the amount spent by them to purchase extra raw material for compensation. It is evident that the boys are more efficient

Table 4.12: Respondents by Managing Insufficient Raw Materials Background and Sex

Sl. No.	Amount spent shortage of raw material	No. of respondents							
		Rural			Urban			Grand Total	
		Boys	Girls	Total	Boys	Girls	Total	Boys	Girls
1.	Rs. 5 - 10	12 (85.72)	233 (64.35)	235 (65.28)	14 (87.50)	84 (67.74)	98 (70.00)	26 (86.67)	307 (65.32)
2.	Rs. 10 – 14	2 (14.28)	123 (35.65)	125 (34.72)	2 (12.50)	40 (32.26)	42 (30.00)	4 (13.33)	163 (34.68)
	Total	14 (100)	316 (100)	360 (100)	16 (100)	124 (100)	140 (100)	30 (100)	470 (100)

Average (Median) amount spent by rural child workers for purchasing of raw materials = Rs. 9.56

Average (Median) amount spent by rural child workers for purchasing of raw materials = Rs. 9.45

Average (Median) amount spent by boys for purchasing of raw materials = Rs. 8.9

Average (Median) amount spent by girls for purchasing of raw materials = Rs. 9.7

Relationship between the background of the child workers and amount spent on shortage of raw materials (X^2 = 1.00 df = 1 P > 0.05)

Relationship between the sex of the child workers and amount spent on shortage of raw material (X^2 = 5.78 df = 1 P < 0.05)

Amount Spent on Shortage of Raw Materials by Sex

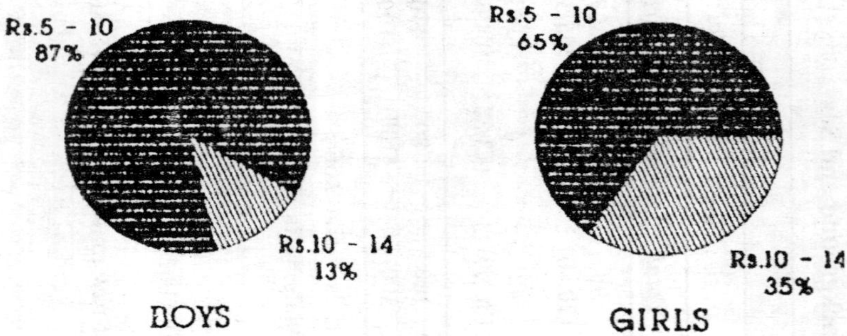

Figure 4.4

than the girls because the former spend less than what the latter spend on the shortage of raw material.

A girl who is 13 years old, narrates the problems in the beediworks as follows:

> I have been doing the beediworks for the last six years. Everyday I have to work for 8 – 10 hours for making 1,000 beedis. For that, they supply 450 – 475 gms. of tendu leaves instead of 500 gms. and 160 – 180 gms. of tobacco dust instead of 500 gms. They supply poor quality and under weighed leaves and moistened tobacco dust. Only few companies supply the right quantity and good quality raw material. On an average, I have to buy extra raw material for Rs. 8 –10 to make 1,000 beedis. If I demand the right quantity and good quality raw material, the contractors scold me and cut the supply of raw material for few days. We depend upon the income from the beediworks for the sustenance of our family. So, we are not able to oppose this practice of the contractors. Besides, a contractor would misbehave with me. While supplying raw material he would touch my hand and body. If I do not tolerate his behaviour, he would not supply the correct quantity and good quality of raw material. At least he expects me to please him with an artificial smile. Somehow, I have been trained to reckon with him because of the need to survive.

Thus besides the punishment by their parents, the children especially the girls above 12 years of age are subject to harassment by the contractors. They are ill-treated at the time of submitting the finished beedis and receiving the raw material. The employees in beedi companies expect to be respected by the beediworkers. They also want the girl children to be jovial while approaching them. Otherwise, several beedis would be removed from the bundles as faulty ones. And also they will supply poor quality and underweighed tendu leaves and tobacco dust. So, a great majority of the working children desire to be relieved from this work. The children have certain aspiration as to what they want to be in future. This is shown in table 4.13.

It is observed that in rural and urban areas over 85 per cent of the children are not willing to continue the beediworks. Among there are more rural boys than girls. None of the urban boys prefer to do this work in future. However, 10 per cent of rural girls and 20 per cent of urban girls like to do the work in future. They think that the beediworks will be their only support for their livelihood. More girls than boys want to be teachers. On the contrary, more boys than girls want to acquire technical skill and get self-employment.

It is clear from the discussions had with the beedi making children that they are willing to do some other work in order to be relieved of the beediworks. A majority of the children are willing to learn the making of plastic wire bags instead of continuing with the beediworks. More urban boys than their rural counterparts are willing to acquire skills in mechanical and electrical work. And the proportion of girls who want to acquire skills is less than the proportion of boys who do so because the boys prefer to go out of their place for their employment, whereas the girls normally do not go to that level.

Table 4.13: Respondents by their Future Aspirations, Background and Sex

Sl. No.	Future aspirations	No. of respondents							
		Rural			Urban			Grand Total	
		Boys	Girls	Total	Boys	Girls	Total	Boys	Girls
1.	No idea	4 (28.57)	52 (15.02)	56 (15.56)	1 (6.25)	41 (33.06)	42 (30.00)	5 (16.67)	93 (19.79)
2.	Teacher	1 (7.14)	167 (48.27)	168 (46.66)	2 (12.50)	20 (16.13)	22 (15.72)	3 (10.00)	187 (39.79)
3.	Self employment	2 (14.26)	7 (2.02)	9 (2.50)	6 (37.50)	2 (1.61)	8 (5.71)	8 (26.67)	9 (1.91)
4.	To continue beediworks	1 (7.14)	35 (10.12)	36 (10.00)	-	25 (20.16)	25 (17.85)	1 (3.52)	60 (12.77)
5.	To learn technical skill	4 (28.57)	52 (15.03)	56 (15.56)	4 (25.00)	26 (20.97)	30 (21.43)	8 (26.67)	78 (16.60)
6.	To be good housewives	-	4 (1.16)	4 (1.11)	-	1 (0.81)	1 (0.71)	-	5 (1.05)
7.	Others	2 (4.29)	29 (8.38)	31 (8.61)	3 (18.75)	9 (7.25)	12 (8.57)	5 (16.67)	38 (8.09)
	Total	14 (100)	346 (100)	360 (100)	16 (100)	124 (100)	140 (100)	30 (100)	470 (100)

Amount Spent on Shortage of Raw Materials by Sex

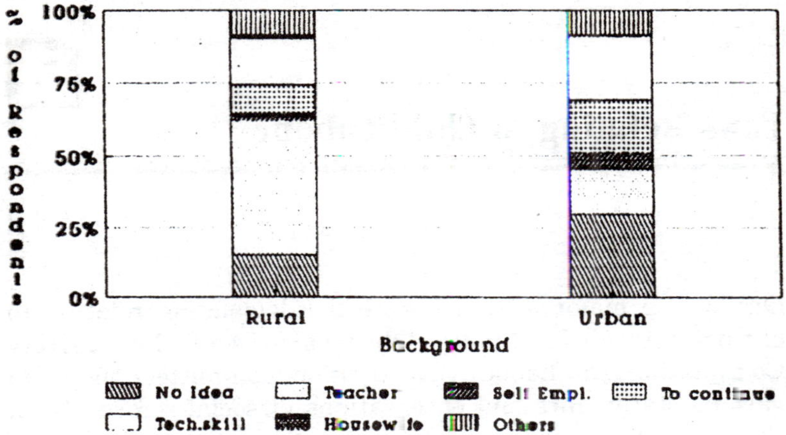

Figure 4.5

REFERENCES

1. G.S. Madan, "Review of Legal Provisions relating to facilities for and working conditions of employed children—the impact of their health, education and development", quoted in Kulshreshtha, *Child work in India*, p. 12.

2. *Report of National Commission on Labour*, 1969, p. 386.

3. Addam Jane, *Child Labour and Paunerism* quoted in *Child Labour in India,* Kulshreshtha, p. 18.

5

Laws Relating to Child Labour

One of the major areas of protective legislation relating to children is child labour. Observations of the Whitely Commission, the Labour Investigation Committee, 1946 and various statements and observations of social reformers on the evils of existing child labour depriving the children of education and health, influenced the framers of Indian Constitution. Therefore, one of the main objectives of the Constitution is the protection of children from adverse effects on their physical and mental development.

Various legislations have been enacted both by the Central and State Governments to mitigate the problems of child labour in tune with the directives of the Indian Constitution. The most comprehensive legislation in this regard has been the Children Labour Prohibition and Regulation Act, 1986. The present chapter deals with the features of different Acts which aim at eradicating the exploitation of the child labourers, with an evaluative study of government policy.

Even before independence, the pinch of the problem of child labour had been felt. The growing concern about this social problem was instrumental in evoking various measures to combat the problem. Historically, the problem received attention over a century ago when the Indian Factories Act, 1881 provided among other things, safeguard for children employed in factories. The Act prohibited the employment of children below seven years. Their working hours were restricted to nine hours per day. The children were to be given four holidays in a month and rest at intervals.

The Act of 1881 covered only factories employing 100 or more persons. The coverage was quite inadequate. But the Act could not be enforced properly and child could not be protected from exploitation. However, the Indian Factories Act was amended from time to time. The year 1920 marked a milestone in the history of child labour laws as the Indian Factories Act was amended in order to incorporate the recommendation of the International Labour Convention for fixing up the minimum age for admitting children into employment and the duration of work for women and children. The definition of the factory was expanded to cover any premises where twenty or more persons were employed and mechanised power was used. The work time hour of children was limited by this Act to six hours a day with an interval of half-an-hour to the children employed for more than 5.5 hours. The children were required by this Act to have a medical certificate regarding their age and physical fitness for the employment.

In the 1920's and 1930's, a series of Acts were passed for the protection of children. The Factories Act which was amended in 1922, raised the age limit to fifteen years. Similarly, the Indian Mines Act of 1923 raised the minimum age for employment in mines to thirteen years.

The Royal Commission on Labour, appointed in 1933, examined the practice of parents pledging the labour of their children by taking advances in return of bonds. A child is defined as a persons who is under fifteen years of age. A parent or guardian making an agreement to pledge the labour of a child is subject to a fine upto Rs. 50. The Act also states that whoever makes an agreement of pledging with the parent or guardian of a child shall be punished with fine upto Rs. 200. A civilised society does not need such a law but the justification for this is that in India due to abject poverty the parents may be constrained to pledge their children for labour and such a practice existed in some parts of the country in the past. The Government of India did not ban the pledging of child labour by parents, but it eliminated the system of indenture, under which adults pledged their own labour on contract.

The Employment of Children Act, 1938, was the first Act introduced to regulate child labour. The main object of the act is "to check the abuses arising out of employment in workshops which are outside the scope of factory legislation". The Act prohibits the employment of children below the age of fifteen in any occupation connected with the transport of passengers, goods or mails by railway, or connected with a port authority within the limits of any port. The Act further laid down that with the exception of children employed as apprentices or trainees, no child between the age of fifteen and seventeen can be employed or permitted to work or engage in the occupation unless he is allowed a rest interval of twelve consecutive hours a day. The penalty for the breach of the act is imprisonment upto one month or fine upto Rs. 500 or both.

However, it is noteworthy that before Independence, the law pertaining to the employment of children in various sectors failed to achieve its goal-the elimination of the evils of child labour. No laws with regard to child labour in agriculture, un-regulated workshops, shops and commercial establishments, were passed.

The Labour Investigation Committee, in its report of 1946, remarked that the main cause of failure of the Acts was the inadequacy of the inspecting staff to enforce the provisions of the laws. The focus on protecting the children from adverse effects of their employment on their physical and mental development, was more progressively sharpened, particularly after Independence. Recognizing the need for special protection to children the makers of the Indian Constitution, made a few provisions to that end. Article 15 permits the State to make any special provision for women and children.

Article 24 states that "no child below the age of 14 shall be employed to work in any factory or mine or engaged in any other hazardous employment".

It is relevant to mention Article 23 here. It says that traffic in human beings, beggars and other similar forms of forced labour is prohibited.

Article 39 expresses that the state shall direct its policy affirming that "children are not abused and that citizens are not forced by economic necessity to enter avocations unsuited to their age or strength, that children are given opportunities and facilities to develop in a healthy manner and in conditions of freedom and dignity, and that childhood or youth are protected against exploitation and against moral and material abandonment".

With a view to eradicating child labour, a good deal of legislation has been done from time to time regulating the employment of children and their working conditions. After independence, the first step taken against exploitation of child labour was the amendment of the Factories Act, 1948.

The Factories Act, 1948 prohibits employment of a child below 14 years in any factory. To safeguard the health of young persons above 4 years of age and below 18 years the Act places a few other restrictions on their employment (with regard to working hours of these young persons). The significant item of the Act, are enumerated below.

According to section 2 (c) of the Factories Act, 1948 "child" means a person who has not completed his fifteen years of age. Section 22 (2) sys that no young prson shall be allowed to clean, lubricate or adjust any part of the prime mover or of any transmission machinery in motion. The cleaning, lubrication or adjustment would expose the young person to risk or injury from any moving part of that machine. Section 27 says that no child shall be employed in any part of a factory for pressing cotton in which a cotton opener is at work provided that if the feed-end of a cotton opener is in a room separated from the delivery-end by a partition extending to the root or to such height as the inspector may be employed on the side of the partition where the feed-end is situated. Section 67 says that no child who has not completed his 14 years shall be required or allowed to work in any factory. Section 71 (a) states that no child shall be employed or permitted to work in any factory for more than four hours a day. Section 71 (b) insists that no child shall be employed or permitted to work in any factory during night.

According to section 2 (a) of the Minimum Wages Act, 1948, "child" means a person who has not completed his fifteen years of age.

Minimum Wages (Central) Rules, 1950, section 24 says that the number of hours which shall constitute a normal working day shall be four and half hours in the case of a child.

Section 2 (e) of the Mines Act, 1952 says that "child" means a person who has not completed his fifteenth year. Section 45 (1) says no child shall be employed in any mine, nor shall any child be allowed to be present in any part of mine which is below ground or in any open cast working in which any mining operation is being carried on.

The Beedi and Cigar Workers Act of 1966 prohibited the employment of children under 14 in any factory manufacturing beedis of cigars.

The Child Labour (Prohibition and Regulation) Act, 1986, is the culmination of the process of consideration that government has been given to this pervasive problem of child labour. This is an Act that prohibits the engagement of children in certain employments and regulates the conditions of child labour in certain other employments.

Since the First International Child Labour Convention (1919), which saw working children in terms of wage employment in formal-sector manufacturing, the world's position on child labour has evolved and expanded over the years. It highlights non-industrial work by children, and most recently, prohibits any kind of work, paid or unpaid, that is injurious to children, and to set out and protection for children who work. State parties in the convention on the Rights of the Child, for example, are required to provide a minimum age for admission to employment "having regard to the relevant provisions of other international instruments" (Article 32).

The laws outlined below are international landmarks in protecting children:

Minimum Age (Industry) Convention No. 5, framed at the first session of the International Labour Organisation (ILO) and ratified by 72 countries, established 14 years as the minimum age for children to be employed in any industry. It was the first international effort to regulate children's participation in the work place and was followed by numerous ILO instruments applicable to other economic sectors.

ILO Forced Labour Convention No. 29 suppresses the use of forced or compulsory labour in all its forms. The term "forced or compulsory labour" is considered to mean all work or service extracted from any person under the threat of penalty and for which they have not offered themselves voluntarily.

International Covenant on Civil and Political Rights was formulated by the UN General Assembly in 1966 and entered into force in 1976. It reaffirms the principles of the Universal Declaration of Human Rights (1948) with regard to civil and political rights. It induces or encourages State parties to help realize these rights. Article 8 states that no one should be kept in slavery or servitude or be required to perform forced or compulsory labour.

International Convent on Economic, Social and Cultural Rights, adopted by the UN General Assembly in 1966 and entered into force in 1976, reaffirms the principles of the Universal Declaration of Human Rights with regard to economic, social and cultural rights. Article 10 enjoins States parties to protect young people from economic exploitation and from employment in work harmful to their physical, moral and mental lives. It also commits State parties to set age limits by which child labour can be prohibited and punished by law.

ILO Minimum Age Convention No. 138 supersedes prior instruments applicable to limited economic sectors. The Convention obliges member States to pursue a national policy designed to ensure the effective abolition of child labour. In this connection, it establishes that no child can be employed in any economic sector below the age designated for the completion of compulsory schooling, that is, below 15 years. The minimum age for admission to any work likely to jeopardize health, safety or moral is 18 years.

Minimum Age Recommendation No. 146 calls States to raise the minimum age of employment to 16 years. Though not legally obligating, it is nonetheless a strong call to action on the part or the member States. Convention No. 138 and this recommendation are regarded as the most comprehensive international instruments and statements on child labour.

Convention on the Rights of the Child, enshrines as interdependent and indivisible, the full range of the civil, political, economic, social and cultural rights of all children that are vital to their survival, development, protection and participation in the lives of their societies. Because of this connection between children's rights and their survival and development, virtually all the Convention's Articles address issues such as education, health nutrition, rest and relaxation, social security and the responsibilities of parents are all related to child labour and its effects on children. One of the tenets of the Convention is that in all actions concerning children, their best interests should be taken into consideration and children should be protected from work that threatens their health, education or development and enjoins State parties to set the minimum age for employment.

ILO proposes for discussion a new convention on hazardous child labour or the elimination of the most intolerable forms of child labour. The Government of India has ratified 6 of the 18 conventions adopted by the International Labour Organisation for children and young persons.

The Minimum Age Convention (No. 138) of 1973 is one of the most significant in that it prescribed the minimum age as not less than 15 years for developed countries and fourteen years for initial fixation by developing countries. For hazardous occupations, the minimum age fixed is 18 years.

A Child Labour Cell which was originally set up in 1979 to serve the M.S. Gurupada Swamy Committee on child labour is now a part of the regular ministry. It is associated with the formulation, co-ordination and implementation of policies and progerammes for the welfare of child labour. The Child Labour Cell is involved in the welfare of children at work through government and non-government action.

The Child Labour Cell grants financial assistance to voluntary organisations to take up action-oriented projects for child labour. These projects would aim at measures to maintain the health of the child while at work by providing supplementary nutrition, non-formal education and vocational training to help them better their employment.

In pursuance of one of the recommendations of the committee on child labour, the Central Advisory Board, which was set up in March, 1981, has been re-constituted in July, 1987 under the Chairmanship of the Minister of Labour to render advice on the problems of child labour. The following were the terms of reference:

1. Review the implementation of the existing legislations administered by the Central Government.

2. Suggest legislative measure as well as welfare measures for the welfare of working children.

3. Review the progress of welfare measures for working children.

4. Recommend the industries and areas where there must be a progressive elimination of child labour.

Keeping in view the fact that legislation alone would not be sufficient to tackle the problem of exploitation of child labour, the government has formulated the National Policy on Child Labour which was announced in Parliament in August, 1987. The action plan under the National Child Labour Policy is set out under the following three heads:

1. The Legislative Action Plan.
2. The focusing of general development programmes for benefiting child labour wherever possible.
3. Project-based plan of action in areas of high concentrations of child labour engaged in wage/ quasi-wage employment.

In addition to the Central Government's Acts, State Governments also passed Acts regulating the conditions of work for young people in restaurants, hotels and shops setting the age limit ranging between 12 and 15 years.

As the year 1979 was announced as the International Year of the Child, the Government of India appointed a committee to analyse the prevailing legislation on child labour. The committee decided that 15 years shall be the minimum age for entering into any employment. But, the government rejected the decision. At the same time, it agreed with certain recommendations like (a) Improving conditions for working children, (b) Health schemes in areas with a concentration of child labour, (c) Supplementary nutrition provided by employers to working children with tax concessions from the government and (d) The establishment of non-formal education for working children.

In his speech in Parliament in 1993, Mr. Sangma, then Union Minister for Labour said that the government has a tremendous responsibility in abolishing child labour as a populist measures. According to him, ban on child labour would trouble the economic conditions of their dependents. So, it would not be advisable to abolish child labour.

The amendment in the Minimum Wages Act ensures that both adult and child workers should be paid equal wages. Moreover, it emphasised that children should be allowed only in non-hazardous jobs and that their job conditions should be regulated.

After a day long consultation with labour ministers from State, Mr. Sangma said that an autonomous body—National Authority for Elimination of Child Labour—would be set up at the country level. The Labour Minister would be the chairman secretary of related Central Ministries and the and the Planning Commission would be its members. The Chief Ministers, particularly from those states where there is a high concentration of child labour, would also be made members of the body. Similarly, Members of Parliament representing such areas would also be associated with it.

After conducting a series of meeting in August 1994, the Labour Ministry has intended to achieve the goal of liberating and rehabilitating atleast two million children working in hazardous industries out of the country's twenty million child labour force. However, the remaining eighteen million working children are not in immediate need of rehabilitation as they are working largely with their parents. Therefore, there is not much of a possibility of their being exploited like their counterparts employed in the manufacturing sector.

On 12 December, 1994 the Minister informed that the government had already proposed to amend the Minimum Wages Act to provide equal wages to adult and child workers thereby discouraging the employment of children. He said that the amendment to he introduced in Parliament, would also stipulate less hours of work for a child worker against an adult worker. However, he points out that the government is confident of eliminating child labor atleast in hazardous industries by the end of the 20th century.

National Child Labour Policy has been set up by the Union Ministry of Labour in 1987 to rehabilitate the child workers. These projects cover (a) the carpet, glass and brassware industries in Uttar Pradesh, (b) the carpet industry in Bihar, (c) the beedi-rolling industry in Orissa, (d) the slate and pencil industry in Madhya Pradesh, (e) slate and tile industry in Andhra Pradesh and (f) the match and fire works industry in Tamil Nadu. The Ministry also extends financial support to non-governmental organisations to undertake action-oriented programmes to tackle the problem of child workers.

In 1990, the United Nations Convention on the Rights of Children 1990 provided an opportunity to respect children's rights and welfare universal. The Government of India has also taken various policies and decisions to try and ensure a better life for children. Besides, various state legislatures have also passed laws for regulating the conditions of employment of children. But, the enforcement of laws is rather inadequate. Therefore, setting a high-level National Commission with powers to supervise the various laws concerning children labour, is a pre-requisite for giving a new dimension to the problem of child labour.

For effective implementation of the action plan, three important points were suggested (a) All concessions and incentives given to industries should be withdrawn, (b) The district magistrate should be empowered to that action against the units found violating the relevant laws.

(c) National Child Labour Elimination Authority should to monitor the implementation of multi-crore schemes.

The Concerned for Working Children (CWC), a Bangalore based organisation, presented in November, 1985 a bill on Child Labour (Employment, Regulation, Training and Development). The bill enlisted the hazardous occupations. But, the list of such occupations was drawn almost entirely from the Employment of Children Act of 1938 and failed to include new hazardous occupations. Also it was not clear about the conception of the term "hazardous". For instance, "rag picking" is not classified as a hazardous work though a number of children who collect scraps of iron, glass, paper and rags often pick up bits of food to eat and are prone to tetanus and skin diseases.

The countries which show total inaction in dealing with child labour will be in course of time given pressure by the Western nations. India seems to be the prime target in this regard. The United States and Germany decided to stop important goods from industries employing child labour. India is also very much particular about liberating children from involuntary labour.

To improve the working conditions of children in the beediworks, the Supreme Court has recently given the verdict that everyone including child workers should be insured for a minimum amount of Rs. 50,000. The premium will be paid by the respective employers. The Court also directed the Regional Provident Fund Commissioner for the implementation in the relevant statute in the areas where beedi units are located.

The Court also recommends implementation of the provision of the Child Labour Abolition Act, 1986. A few directions to regulate the working conditions of the workers in beedi units by the Bench are listed below:

1. The labour laws including the Beedi and Cigar Workers Act should be strictly enforced to ensure the workers' legitimate' rights.

2. A government labour establishment should be set up in the area to answer the requirements of the matter.

3. Abiding by the Beedi and Cigar Workers' Rules, the system of furnishing pass-books to the home workers would be eliminated.

4. Instead, great care should be taken to ensure the maintenance of "the register system".

5. The beneficial provisions of the Beedi Workers' Welfare Cell Act, 1976 and the Beedi Workers' Welfare Act, 1976 should be made operational in the area because these two Acts are the legislations of the Central Government.

6. The "Pass-books" should properly be maintained in the name of actual workers.

7. The welfare fund should properly be administrated and in the case of the death of a workman, appropriate assistance should be extended out of the fund as early as possible.

India by its new legislation, legalised child labour in non-hazardous employment. This appeared to be a violation of the International Labour Organisation Convention on Child Labour. But, at the international level, India's new strategy of regulation of child labour rather than abolition was well supported by the officials of the International Labour Organisation.

The important recommendations for the intervention of the states in "Jury verdict" on child labour are listed as follows:

1. The Government of India being a party to the U.N. Conventions on the Right of the Child (CRC), there is need to amend Article 24 of the Indian Constitution to confirm with Article 1 of the CRC which defines a child as upto 18 years of age. The Constitution clearly sanctions the prohibition of

employment of children in all areas and in all forms.

2. Along with this all other related labour laws should be strictly implemented. Child labour can not be categorised as 'hazardous' or 'non-hazardous'. Any form of child labour is hazardous for the healthy growth of children. The hazardous—non-hazardous dichotomy for children is a non-reality.

3. Pending amendments of the 1986 Act, the Supreme Court judgement (1996) in the case of M.C. Mehta Vs. Government of Tamil Nadu is to be strictly implemented by the Government of Tamil Nadu.

4. While poverty is cited as an alibi for child labour, millions of children in the work force perpetuate poverty and a vicious cycle is at work. Many developing countries with much less resources than India much higher levels of employment of children.

In this context, the following strategies are recommended for implementation:

1. More employment opportunities and income generation avenues should be created for adults. All development programmes and anti-poverty schemes should be targeted on child labour households.

2. Enforcement of minimum wages for an adult worker without any gender discrimination.

3. The most important issue is to provide free, compulsory and quality education for all children of school-going age. The Supreme Court has held in the Mohini Jain and Unni Krishnan cases that primary education is a fundamental right and is justifiable. This should be strictly enforced. In this regard, the Tamil Nadu Compulsory Primary Education Act (1994) passed by the State Assembly

should come into force atleast from the academic year of 1998-'99.

4. There should be adequate budgetary allocation for compulsory primary education n the state and for the abolition of child labour with proper plan of action and target setting.[1]

National Convention on Child Labour recommended that no child below the age of 14 should be allowed to work in hazardous or non-hazardous industries and primary education should be made free and compulsory. A panel of judges, after hearing testimonies of child labourers from 11 sectors suggested that penalty should be imposed on employers of child labour. They regretted that even after 50 years of independence, children continue to be employed in hazardous industries. They felt that there should exist no classification of hazardous or non-hazardous industries as all of them are dangerous for children. The panel comprising Prof. Muchkund Dubey, Justice Leila Seth, Justice Rajinder Sachar, Mr. T.S. Shankaran, Prof. Yash Pal, Mr. N. Ram, Ms. Indira Jaisingh and Mr. R. Venkata Raman unanimously demanded free education, health care, social protection and complete abolition of child labour.

They said the prevailing law regarding child labour was not adequate enough to ensure completing abolition cf child labour. It should be amended accordingly to make it more effective. Although the Constitution provides education to all, the government has failed to implement the law properly in the country. Therefore, the panel felt and suggested that the states should formulate their own law in an effort to eliminate child labour completely.

The Supreme Court gave directions regarding child labour to the states concerned. They are listed below:

1. A survey would be made of the aforesaid type of child labour which would be completed within six months from the date of implementation.

2. Top start with, work could be taken up regarding those employments which have been mentioned in Article 24, which may be regarded as core sector, to determine which hazardous aspect of the employment would be taken as criterion. The most hazardous employment may rank first in priority, to be followed by comparatively less hazardous ones and so on. It may be mentioned here that the National Children Labour Policy as announced by the Government of India has already identified some industries for priority action, and the industries identified are given below.

   (a) The match industry in Sivakasi, Tamil Nadu.

   (b) The diamond polishing industry in Surat, Gujarat.

   (c) The precious stone polishing industry in Jaipur, Rajasthan.

   (d) The glass industry in Firozabad, Uttar Pradesh.

   (e) The braass-ware industry in Moradabad, Uttar Pradesh.

   (f) The handmade carpet industry in Mirzapur-Bhadohi, Uttar Pradesh.

   (g) The lock-making industry in Aligarh, Uttar Pradesh.

   (h) The slate industry in Markapur, Andhra Pradesh.

   (i) The slate industry in Mandsaur, Madhya Pradesh.

3. The employment to be given as per the direction of the Supreme Court could be dovetailed to other assured employment. On this being done, it is apparent that its direction would not require generation of much additional employment.

4. The employment so given could as well be the industry where the child is employed, a public undertaking and would be manual in nature in as much as the child in question must be engaged in doing manual work. The undertaking chosen for employment shall be one which is nearest to the place of residence of the family.

5. In those cases where alternative employment would not be made available as aforesaid, the parent/guardian of the child concerned would be paid the income which would be earned on the corpus, which would be a sum of Rs. 25,000 for each child, every month. The employment given or payment made would cease to be operative if the child is not sent by the parent/guardian for education.

6. On discontinuation of the employment of the child, his education would be assured in a suitable institution with a view to making him a better citizen. It may be pointed out that Article 45 mandates compulsory free education for all children until they complete the age of 14 years. It would be the duty of the Inspectors to see that this call of the Constitution is carried out.

7. A district could be the unit of collection so that the executive head of the district keeps a watchful eye on the work of the inspectors. Further, in view of the magnitude of the task, a separate cell in the Labour Department of the appropriate Government would be created. Monitoring of the scheme would also be necessary and the Secretary of the Department could perhaps do this work. Overall monitoring by the Ministry of Labour, government of India, would be beneficial and worthwhile.

8. The Secretary to the Ministry of Labour, Government of India would appraise this Court within one year from the day of judgement about

the compliance of the aforesaid directions. If the petitioner would need any further or other order in the light of the compliance report, it would be open to him to do so.

9. The Court observes that on the directions given being carried out, penal provision contained in the above noted 1986 Act would be used where employment of child labour, prohibited by the Act, would be found

10. In so far as the non-hazardous jobs are concerned, the Inspector shall have to see that the working hours of the child are not more than four to six hours a day and he/she receives education at least for two hours each day. It would also be seen that the entire cost of education is borne by the employer.[2]

Inspite of all these efforts taken by the government, this problem continue to exist. In connection with this, it is relevant to mention that there is a contradiction between the Articles 24,39 and 45 of the Indian Constitution which deal with the rights of children, and the Child Labour (Prohibition and Regulation) Act, 1986. In other words, this Act violates the Indian Constitution. According to the Articles 24 and 39 of the Indian Constitution, no child below 14 years of age shall be employed in any factory or mine or engaged in hazardous employment. They should not be forced by economic necessity to enter avocations unsuited to their age or strength. But, this Act while emphasizing the prohibition of child labour, justifies the regulation of this system, i.e. regulating the working conditions of child labour. This contradiction would rather complicate the issues relating to child labour as either the country would categorically or decide to regulate the working condition of the children engaged in various jobs. Therefore, this Act has to be modified according to the Constitution so as to arrive at a uniform prescription that this problem will be eradicated once for all.

PARENTS' KNOWLEDGE ABOUT LEGISLATION ON CHILD LABOUR

When the parents of child workers were asked about their knowledge regarding the employment of children below the age of 14 years in the beediworks, a large majority of them were found to be ignorant of the law that employing children in beediworks is an offence. This is presented in table 5.1.

Table 5.1: Respondents' by their Knowledge of Employment Children and Background

Sl. No.	*Employment of Children below 14 years of age*	*No. of respondents*		
		Rural	*Urban*	*Total*
1.	Offence	32 (8.89)	3 (2.14)	35 (7.00)
2.	Not Offence	328 (91.11)	137 (97.86)	465 (93.00)
	Total	360 (100)	140 (100)	500 (100)

A reading of the above table show that of the total number of parents, only 7 per cent of them know that employment of children below 14 years of age is an offence and 93 per cent of them are ignorant of this. Of the total number of rural parents, 8.89 per cent of them know this as an offence and 91.11 per cent of them do not know of it. Of the total number of urban parents, only 2.14 per cent of them know it as an offence and 97.86 per cent of them do not know of it.

It is clear that an overwhelming majority (over 90 per cent) of rural and urban parents are ignorant that employing children below 14 years of age is an offence. The reason is that they are illiterates. However, a limited number of parents know it as an offence. This shows that the enforcement machinery is rather inactive. It is also clear that from enacting the legislation to ensuring its effective enforcement seems to be a long and difficult process in contemporary situation in which alarming proportions of boys and girls are absorbed into work force every day.

This view is supported by the general opinion among the parents of child work force in beediworks that employing one's son or daughters below the age of 14 years is in no way undesirable in the sense that it provides supplementary income to their family. It is relevant here to refer to the statement of a mother:

> My husband is a drunkard. He spends all the money that he earns every day from his work. Since he can not be corrected, I have to bear with his indifferent behaviour. My earnings from the beediworks are not sufficient to meet the basic needs of our family. Under such circumstances, I have no other go except to employ my daughter in the beediworks. If I had not done it on time, I could not have saved my family from starvation. Therefore, I do not consider the act of employing my daughter in the beediworks as illegal.

BEEDIWORKS AND LABOUR LAWS

Generally, the beedi workers in the areas surveyed are not much exposed to labour laws. Instead, they are subject to economic exploitation. Since a majority of them are illiterates, they are ignorant of the labour laws. Some of them know about one or two aspects of few labour laws about not in details. The table 5.2 shows the awareness of parents regarding labour laws.

The table 5.2 clearly shows that, by and large, the beedi workers in the rural areas do not know of any law relating to child labour. In the urban areas, only four out of 140 parents know one or two Acts relating to child labour. Those who know the laws are least concerned about them. The parents express that they have no time to think about the legal aspect of child labour. Their only concern is rolling the maximum number of beedis within the stipulated time. Since the are, by and large depending upon the beediworks for

Table 5.2: Parents' by their Awareness of Laws Relating to Child Labour and Background

Sl. No.	Various Legal Measures	No. of respondents					
		Rural			Urban		
		Aware	Not aware	Total	Aware	Not aware	Total
1.	Minimum Wages Act, 1948	—	360 (100)	360 (100)	1 (0.71)	139 (99.29)	140 (100)
2.	Beedi & Cigar Workers Act, 1966	—	360 (100)	360 (100)	1 (0.70)	139 (99.29)	140 (100)
3.	Beedi Workers Welfare Fund Act, 1976	—	360 (100)	360 (100)	—	140 (100)	140 (100)
4.	Child Labour Prohibition Act, 1986	—	360 (100)	360 (100)	—	140 (100)	140 (100)
5.	Factories Act, 1948	—	360 (100)	360 (100)	—	140 (100)	140 100)
6.	Payment of Bonus Act, 1965	—	360 (100	360 (100)	1 (0.71)	139 (99.29)	140 (100)
7.	Workmen's Compensation Act, 1923	—	360 (100)	360 (100)	—	140 (100)	140 (100)
8.	Employees' State Insurance Act, 1948	—	360 (100)	360 (100)	1 (0.71)	139 (99.29)	140 (100)
9.	Provident Fund Act, 1952	—	360 (100)	360 (100)	—	140 (100)	140 (100)
10.	Industrial Employment Act, 1946	—	360 (100)	360 (100)	—	140 (100)	140 (100)

their earnings, they do not mind whether the act of employing children is illegal or not.

It is important to note that nearly two-thirds of the children were able to get the pass-books only by giving a false age. For instance, a 13 year old boy reported to the beedi contractor that he was 15 years old and got a pass-book on his name. He used to collect raw material from the contractors using all his tact and return the completed beedis. The case is similar with all the children owning pass-books. However, they are not benefited by the provision extended to them by various laws. Thus, they are subject to exploitation along with other adult workers.

In Tirunelveli District, most of the companies pay the minimum wage, but some companies pay less than the prescribed minimum wages including Dearness Allowance for 1,000 beedis. Some companies make payment once in a week or ten days. Some other companies pay the workers at their convenience. In such companies, workers are worried about their payments. A beedi company deducts a nominal amount from the wages as compulsory deposit for their own finance company. It will not be refunded in cash. But, the beedi workers can purchase articles through this finance company and for that they have to pay a high interest to the company. The due amount will be recouped from the deposit. However, there is no interest given for their deposits. But, a meager amount will be paid as bonus. Initially, every worker has to pay a sum of Rs. 100 to start the account in the finance company. People disclose that every week they lose Rs. 8 from their wages. Most of the workers get frustrated because of this sort of exploitation. However, due to lack of employment opportunity and poverty, they are not able to switch over to over jobs.

According to section 26 of the Beedi Cigar Workers' (Conditions of Employment) Act, 1966 a beedi company grants leave wages on the basis of work done. Usually this amount is distributed to the beedi workers by the contractors. But, at the time of distribution, the contractors take 10-20 per cent of the leave wages as their commission and given the remaining amount to the workers after getting their signature for the total amount. In some villages, this sort of commission will go upto 50 per cent. In some other companies, no leave wage is paid, but, signatures are obtained at the time of disbursing the bonus as if the workers had received the bonus.

According to Payment of Bonus Act, 1965 almost all beedi companies should distribute the bonus amount to the workers. But contractors deduct 10-20 pr cent of bonus and pay the remainder to the workers. In some companies, two types of pass-books are maintained. However, bonus is calculated on only one pass-book account. Therefore, the workers get 50 or below 50 per cent of bonus. But, signature is obtained for the full amount of bonus. In some other, companies, there is an inordinate delay in the payment of bonus. Such malpractices can be stopped if the principal employer deals with the workers directly. If this is the plight of the adults, the child workers have a rare chance of getting the benefits extended for their welfare.

According to Beedi Workers' Welfare Fund Act, 1976 some companies provide various welfare facilities to the beedi workers and their children. It provides education loan facility, scholarship and maternity benefit. Both in rural and urban areas, most of the companies provide scholarships to the beedi workers' child. Very few companies deny them such facilities. But, loan facilities and maternity benefits are extended to the workers including children.

Some of the beedi companies follow the rule of Provident Fund Act 1952. Accounts are properly maintained where the principal employer deals with the workers directly. In the case of contract agencies, some contractors are maintaining accounts properly. Some others do not do so. Two pass-books are maintained in beedi company to enter the number of beedis done in a day. Account for three or four days in a week is not entered in the original pass-book. Therefore, for these days there is no Provident Fund contribution from the employers. But, employees' contribution is deducted from their wages. If the worker enquires the contractor after three or four years about the Provident Fund, a majority of the contractors/beedi companies tell them that they have no money in their provident fund account. But, the beedi workers do not have proper evidence (pass-book entry regarding Provident Fund contribution) to prove it otherwise. A few contractors/beedi companies properly maintain accounts for the Provident Fund contribution. In some other companies, Provident Fund contribution is properly deducted, but it is not properly deposit. It seems that the labour department has not taken firm action against the contactors/beedi companies for such malpractices.

A girl of 14 years engaged in the beediworks in a village had the following compliant about her employer:

> I have been doing the beediworks for the past six years. Initially, I was working with my mother. Now I have my own pass-book. For the last two years, I have been doing this work in a beedi company. Every day I make 1,000 beedis. I am getting my wage once in a week. At the time of wage distribution, my contractor will enter only 50 per cent of the work done in one pass-book and other 50 per cent of the work in some other pass-book. This is mainly to avoid the payment of bonus. Usually, bonus is calculated on the basis of actual work done. Thus, I can get only 50 per cent of bonus. Similarly, I get only 50 per cent of Provident Fund contribution from the employer instead of cent per cent. I do not get leave salary benefit from my employer. If I ask for the bonus, Provident Fund contribution and leave salary, contractors get irritated and punish us by supplying poor quality of raw material and discarding the beedis as of poor quality. Sometime, they do not supply raw material. Since we completely depend upon this work for earnings, we keep quiet.

Though the government has taken several steps to eliminate child labour, the problem continues to exist. However, the government keep taking efforts. Simultaneously, the government wants to regulate the working conditions of child labour. It is suggested that a separate monitoring unit should be set up to review the adequacy of the prevailing legislation on child labour. The minimum age, minimum wages and pre-conditions for the employment of children should be made in tune with the latest Acts relating to the children.

Working hours, duration of night work and rest interval for the child workers should be taken into account seriously. Most of the units do not have uniform provisions to regulate the working hours of children. This results in the exploitation of child labour. In addition to this, they are subject to health problems. Therefore, uniform legislation with regard to the working hours to children is an urgent need of the hour.

The fixing up of the working hours should not interfere with the children attending schools. If they are more in number, non-formal education system may be organised in their place of work. If the children are not provided with proper schooling, it will add to the problem of child labour. So, compulsory education should be made necessary to tackle the problem. Except in Melapalayam town, the beedi workers in other towns are largely home workers. The prevailing statutes do not make the parents relieve their children from work. The parents should be made aware of the seriousness of the problem and also about the future of children. With the support of the government, various voluntary service organisations should plunge into action to create an awareness among the people about the importance of education for the poor child labourers.

6

Health Problems

Occupational health hazards have been recently given more importance because of the increase in occupational disease. The occupation itself causes a variety of health problems. For instance, the beedi workers are affected by diseases like tuberculosis, chronic bronchitis, nutritional anemia, back pain, head-ache and eye irritation. It is reported that children engaged in beediworks are often object to respiratory infections.

Children are introduced in the beediworks at the age of 7 or 8. After acquiring the skill in the work, they have to work on an average of 10 hours per day. Long hours of working in a particular posture would certainly cause excessive fatigue. It has its adverse effect on the physical development and general health condition of the children. Work pressure makes them weak and also stunts their growth.

It was observed during field work that the age of many working children do not synchronize with their growth. For instance, one would estimate the age of a girl as 7 or 8 just by considering her physical appearance, But, her real age counts as 12 years. This stunted growth of the children is mainly due to malnutrition.

Malnutriton which is mainly responsible for anemia. Affects health, efficiency, earning capacity, intellectual attainment and overall fitness. A project report by G. Karunanithi discloses that since the children engaged in the beediworks have the problem of malnutrition, they are highly susceptible to the respiratory infections resulting in frequent cold and cough. The children suffering from these health problems, are often suspected to have the problem of chronic bronchitis.[1] The present study supports this finding that three-fourths of the children surveyed are affected by respiratory infections because they get exposed to tobacco dust and tendu leaves for most of the time in a day. Tobacco is an irritant that causes irritation in the inner area of the nose and wind pipe and results in frequent cough.

In addition, the small houses that accommodate too many members, are poorly ventilated and unhygienically maintained. In the absence of free ventilation, they inhale the air polluted with tobacco dust. They are thus subject to respiratory infections. The dust also affects their eyes and causes irritation. Almost all the children complain of this problem.

Since the children sit to work for hours together in a particular posture they have back pain. This might even restrict their movements in the long run. The children who work for several hours a day, complain of head-ache. Exposure to tobacco dust makes them prone to chronic cough and tuberculosis. The ignorant parents do not take any effort to get their children treated in time. In this situation, organizing medical camps and follow up are the immediate needs that can save them from such dangerous diseases.

Worm infestation though not reported by the children surveyed, is also one of the serious health problems affecting children mostly living in unhygienic surroundings. It affects the absorption of nutrients especially iron and aggravates the problem of malnutrition and anemia in the children. This results in arresting the growth of children and reducing their weight. Doctors feel that a large number of children engaged in beediworks are also affected by worm infestation due to the lack of personal hygiene and insanitary conditions prevailing in their residential areas.

Anaemia, mostly the disease of the poor, is widely prevalent among the beedi workers. A large majority of the households are affected by lung or respiratory diseases such as tuberculosis and bronchitis. A considerable number of them suffer form back pain and head-ache. Certain diseases affecting the working children are listed here as reported by them and their parents. It is shown in table 6.1.

A large majority of boys and girls are suffering from the respiratory diseases such as chronic bronchitis, primary complex and frequent cold and cough. However, there is no significant difference between the proportion of the boys and girls suffering from this health problem. The problems such as head-ache, back pain and body pain and eye irritation are other major health problems that affect a great majority of the boys and girls. But, the proportion of children suffering from fever and skin disease is rather insignificant.

It is evident fro the analysis that, there is no significant relationship between the sex of the children on the one hand and the diseases on the other. It is obvious that respiratory infection is a common health problem among the children. The ailment of the child workers surveyed, varies from cough to acute tuberculosis. This shows that there is an association between the beediworks and respiratory problem to a notable extent. Therefore, there is an urgent need to organize a series of medical camps in areas where there is lot of child labour.

In a similar way, several epidemiological, experimental and clinical studies indicate a close association between malnutrition and tuberculosis. Clinical studies also point out such an association between severe protein energy malnutrition and tuberculosis in children. However, these observations identify only the association between the two conditions and do not establish the causal relationship.

Some parents of the working children do suffer from chronic bronchitis and tuberculosis. This is due to their entry into the hazardous work at a tender age, long hours of work till mid-night and over crowding in their houses. In the

Table 6.1: Respondents by Diseases and Sex

Sl. No.	Types of diseases	No. of respondents					
		Boys			Girls		
		Suffered	Not Suffered	Total	Suffered	Not Suffered	Total
1.	Respiratory diseases	28 (93.33)	2 (6.67)	30 (100)	402 (85.53)	68 (14.47)	470 (100)
2.	Fever	1 (3.33)	29 (96.67)	30 (100)	66 (14.04)	404 (85.96)	470 (100)
3.	Head-ache	29 (96.67)	1 (3.33)	30 (100)	453 (95.96)	17 (4.04)	470 (100)
4.	Back pain and Body pain	29 (96.67)	1 (3.33)	30 (100)	451 (95.96)	19 (4.04)	470 (100)
5.	Eye irritation	28 (93.33)	2 (6.67)	30 (100)	416 (88.50)	54 (11.50)	470 (100)
6.	Skin disease	1 (3.33)	29 (96.67)	30 (100)	30 (16.38)	440 (93.62)	470 (100)

Respondents Suffered by Diseases

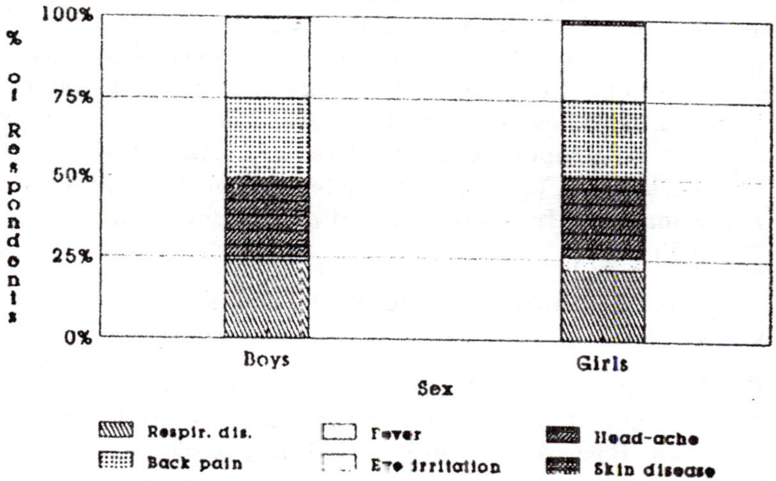

Figure 6.1

course of time, their children also get infected with tuberculosis. Since their parents do not bother about taking special efforts to get their children treated in time, organizing medical camps and follow up is the immediate need to save them from such a dangerous disease.

A doctor in Melapalayam, was interviewed elaborately in order to know the health problems of beedi workers, especially the children. He says:

> Malnutrition is the major cause of many of the health problems among the beedi workers including children. Especially more women of child bearing age and children than men, are affected by the problem of nutritional anaemia. A large number of children engaged in beediworks are also affected by worm infestation due to the lack of personal hygiene and insanitary condition prevailing in their residential areas. Thus, the decrease of their appetite due to worm, infestation would arrest their growth. There are more incidents of TB cases from the beediworks than that of

those from other categories of workers, especially working in such cottage industries. Asthama is another health problem among the beedi workers. The allergy caused by the tobacco dust is mainly responsible for this disease. They work in dim light. Their place of work has no proper ventilation facility. As a result, the workers suffer from eye defects. Due to over strain women are frequently suffering from fever rather than men.

It is relevant here to refer to the statement of a mother who says:

> For the last 32 years I have been doing the beediworks. I have 3 daughters and 2 sons. My husband is a sick man. Basically, we are agricultural workers. But, due to monsoon failure and economic crisis in our family, I shifted to this work. I commenced this work since I was 10 years old. I was making 1,000 beedis per day, for that I work from morning 8.00 a.m. to evening 7.00 p.m. At the age of 25 years, I had allergy problem. Doctor advised me to avoid this work. But, due to our family condition, I could not. At age of 32 I was severely affected by breathing problem. Then, I took treatment from government hospital. Still I undergo the treatment. At the age of 42 I was severely affected by chronic bronchitis. Also I am suffering from backpain and severe headache. Besides, doing the work in dim light in the nights, my eye sight is also affected. But, due to poverty I have to work. Now, I can roll 500 or 750 beedis per day with the help of my daughter. I realise that the beediworks is hazardous to health. I would be very happy if I get a job other than this work.

This clearly reveals that a series to health problems is caused by the beediworks.

A girl of 13 years engaged in the beediworks in a village explains her plight as follows:

In order to complete my prescribed target in a day, I have a to strain for 9-10 hours. I have to sit in one position and concentrate on the beediwork. My thoughts revolve around beedi making. For the past six years I have been doing this work. Now, I am often affected by head ache. Daily I have to take many tablets for this ailment. Sitting in a particular position for hours together, my hip, back and whole body get pain. The allergy caused by tobacco dust is a big problem to me. It causes cough, wheezing and sneezing. I am a fatherless girl. My mother is aged and sick. Hence, I have to do this hazardous work for our survival.

Food

In regard to the diet of the children in rural areas, a majority of them take two meals per day. But, in urban areas, a majority of children take three meals per day. But, it does not mean that the food they consume is adequate and well balanced. This is show in table 6.2.

In rural areas, a majority of boys take three meals per day, but a majority of girls take two meals per day. On the other and, in urban areas, a great majority of boys and girls take three meals. It is clear that the rural girls forego one meal a day but they work to sustain the livelihood of their family. Thus there is a discrimination against sex with regard to the provision of daily food. In other words, more boys than girls would get three meals per day. The significance in the relationship between the sex of the children and number of times in a day they get food is confirmed by a statistical test. The analysis revels that more urban child workers take meals thrice in a day than their rural counterparts. This shows that there is a discrepancy between rural and urban children with respect to the provision of daily food. That is there is a significant relationship between the rural and urban children with respect to number of times in a day they get food. This is proved by a statistical test.

Rice is the main food for both rural and urban beedi workers. In many rural and urban households, it is the only

Table 6.2: Respondents by Number of Meal take in a day, Background and Sex

Sl. No.	Number of mean per day	No. of respondents							
		Rural			Urban			Grand Total	
		Boys	Girls	Total	Boys	Girls	Total	Boys	Girls
1.	Twice	4 (28.57)	193 (55.78)	197 (54.72)	3 (18.75)	12 (9.68)	15 (10.71)	7 (23.33)	205 (43.62)
2.	Thrice	10 (71.43)	153 (44.32)	163 (45.28)	13 (81.25)	112 (90.32)	125 (89.29)	23 (76.67)	265 (56.38)
	Total	14 (100)	346 (100)	360 (100)	16 (100)	124 (100)	140 (100)	30 (100)	470 (100)

Relationship between background of child workers and number of meals in a day (x^2 = 79.93 df = 1 P < 0.05)

Relationship between sex of child workers and number of meals in day (x^2 = 4.74 df = 1 P < 0.05)

Respondents by getting Food in a Day and Background

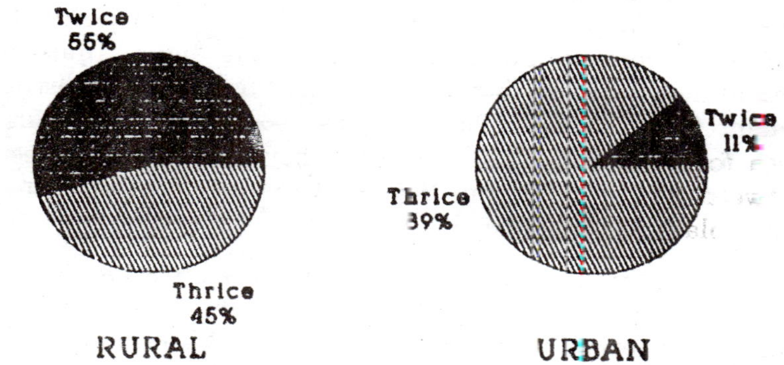

Figure 6.2

Respondents by Getting Food in a Day and Sex

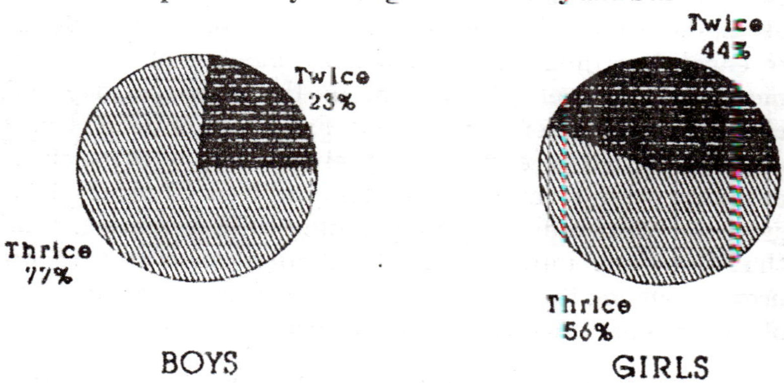

Figure 6.3

item of food for all the three times in a day. Usually, the side dish is vegetable curry or pickle or 'Chutney' (native side dish). A majority of households prepare food in the evening. But, they prepare in excess, because the family member would take full meal in the evening and keep the remaining for the next day. A great majority of respondents in rural households take the previous day meal in the morning and after-noon. Some adults forego break fast in the mornings by taking cup of tea or coffee between 7.00 and 8.00 a.m. A majority of the rural workers go for tea or coffee between 12.30 and 1.30 p.m. But in urban areas, a large majority of the beedi workers and child workers take "idlis" (native eatable item) or any other tiffin called as "nasta" mostly bought from out side. They prepare food in the fore-noon both for noon and night. Usually, they take tea or coffee between 3.30 to 5.00 p.m. But, above 90 per cent of them drink black tea or coffee.

Both in rural and urban areas, the beedi workers take a full meal only once a day. At other times they have half of what they normally eat. Usually, they cook ordinary rice (mostly ration rice) with cheap vegetables. Non-vegetarian food is tasted by the children once a month in rural areas. But, in urban areas, the children take non-vegetarian meal twice or thrice a month. Sometimes both in rural and urban areas, the parents provide non-vegetarian food to the children to encourage them to produce more number of beedis. In most of the households, parents fix the target per day and compel their children to achieve it. From this, one can clearly understand that parents exploit their children by giving them an incentive in terms of non-vegetarian food. Thus, the food system of the beedi workers including child workers reveals that they lack nutrition. And malnutrition is a common problem among the beedi workers; especially, a large number of children are affected by this problem.

For instance, a 11 year old girl engaged in beediworks in a village near Kadayam gave the following report:

> My parents are basically farmers and absolutely unfamiliar to the beediworks. But, then put me to this work due to severe economic crisis in my family. It is not only hard but also painful to sit and do the work for hours together without a break. In addition, the work load is heavy. But, I can earn only Rs. 20-23 per day. I have three younger sisters. My parents go to work wherever they find employment. They don't know

beediworks. My sisters are at tender age. Our family income is very low, so, we take inadequate food just twice a day. I am working from 8 to 10 hours a day.

PHYSICAL ATMOSPHERE

In the areas surveyed, the children are always exposed to polluted atmosphere. One can see that in almost all the households, the ground is littered with the waste beedi leaves. In most of the households, the waste leaves are not cleaned regularly as the household members are busy with beedi making from dawn to dusk. They work, eat and sleep on the uncleaned floor. They do not realize the importance of personal hygiene or cleanliness as they are used to the unhealthy atmosphere in the work place. The other reason for being so is that the beedi workers including the children are busily engaged in their work from early morning to late evening.

The unclean physical atmosphere both inside and outside the house contributes much to the health problem so the beedi workers, especially the children. It is understood that the children are more vulnerable to infectious diseases than the adult workers. Infection has an injurious effect on the growth and development of the children, especially when there is malnutrition. It may also have an adverse affect on mental development.

Housing condition in the areas surveyed is also not good. The houses are in a very poor condition. In urban areas, people are living in congested houses with several members under joint family system. In rural areas, a majority of the people live in huts. Any outsider would find it very difficult to approach the residential area of the beedi workers, especially during the rainy season. Such an insanitary condition is harmful to the health of the children. Therefore, implementing the scheme of group housing is an effective measure to prevent the beedi workers from getting infected diseases.

MEDICAL FACILITIES

The beedi workers go to various types of hospital for treatment. A great majority of them prefer allopathic treatment, but choices differ with regard to the place of treatment. Some of them go to private allopathic hospitals, some others prefer to go to government hospitals and few people receive treatment from Beedi Workers' Welfare Fund Dispensary . In Rural areas, the beedi workers go to various places for medical treatment. But, in urban areas, a large majority of them get treatment from local dispensaries and few people go outside their living place.

In rural area's on the whole, three-fourths of the households have medical treatment within their own village. But, very few households get medical treatment from outside their village. If it is taken for area wise analysis, in Keelapavoor Block, most of them get medical treatment from local private doctors. Very few people go to Beedi Workers' Welfare Fund Dispensary in Pavoorchathram. From their own villages, beedi workers have to cover a distance of 3-7 k.ms. for treatment. In Alangulam Block. A majority of them get medical treatment from the local doctors. Very few people go for Beedi Workers' Welfare Fund Dispensary situated in the town Alangulam. Some others cross a distance of 5-9 k.ms. for treatment. In Pappakudi Block, a majority of the beedi workers get medical treatment from the local Primary Health Centres and private clinics. Some of the workers go to Mukkudal for medical treatment given by Beedi Workers' Welfare Fund Dispensary. For that, they have to travel a distance of 3-5 k.ms. In Kadayam Block, some people get medical treatment from Kadyam Beedi Workers' Welfare Fund Dispensary and some from Mukkudal Beedi Workers' Welfare Fund Dispensary. A majority of the people in the block get treatment from local doctors, because they do not want to travel a distance of 3-7 k.ms. from their native villages.

In Tenkasi Block, a majority of the rural workers receive treatment from their villages. In Tenkasi town, a majority of them go to Beedi Worker's Welfare Fund

Dispensary, some of them go to private clinics and few prefer government hospitals for treatment.

In Melapalayam town, some beedi workers visit Beedi Workers' Welfare Fund Dispensary situated in the town itself. Some other go to private clinics and government hospital. Few of them visit Palayamkottai town for treatment. Beedi Workers' Welfare Fund Dispensary is located in souther part of the town. So, only people from the southern part are willing to go there. There are a number of dispensaries and a few clinics within the town to cater to the needs of the people.

It is imperative that mention should be made of the Beedi Workers' Welfare Fund Dispensary. The Government of India has established such dispensaries in places of high concentration of beedi works. They provide the medical service exclusively to the beedi workers and their family members. However, a majority of the beedi workers go to private clinics for treatment instead of approaching the Beedi Workers' Welfare Fund Dispensary. Perhaps it may be due to the overcrowding of patients in the dispensary both in the morning and in the evening. The beedi workers are very particular in completing the target of a day. So, they are not able to wait for a long time for treatment.

The dispensaries meant for the beedi workers need to be well-equipped in terms of providing them with adequate beds, surgical instruments medicine and other things required for the patients. Unless they are provided adequately they will not be able to save thousands of workers from tuberculosis which is considered one of the most prevalent and diseases. Besides, equipping such dispensaries, the Community Health Workers should be oriented to the development needs of the working children. To meet the medical requirements of TB patients, the Malapalayam town and other villages in the study areas have also to be equipped by providing them with adequate infrastructural facilities through establishing adequate number of Beedi Workers' Welfare Fund Dispensaries.

For instance, a women worker comments on Beedi Workers' Welfare fund Dispensary as follows:

> I have been doing the beediwork over 22 years, every day, I am rolling 1,000 beedis. For that, I have to strain from 7-9 hours besides my household work. At my 36 years of age, I was severely affected by backpain and at 41, I was affected by TB. Doctor advised me to take injections and tablets for a period of time.But, my village is 8 k.ms. away from Alangulam town. So, I was unable to visit Beedi Workers' Welfare Fund Dispensary. At the sametime, I was not able to pay for injections prescribed by a local doctor. So, I am severely affected by TB. It will be helpful to us if some one can arrange to establish a Beedi Workers' Welfare Fund Dispensary in our area so that it would save many workers from this disease.

For instance, a 14 year old child states as follows:

> In Melapalayam town, a majority of the workers are affected by TB and chronic bronochits. Some are affected by backpain. I have the problem of cough due to the allergy caused by tobacco dust. I am also suffering from back ache due to the nature of the work. Since, the Beedi Workers' welfare Fund Dispensary in our town is always crowded. I have to stand in a queue for atleast a couple of hours to take treatment. It is indeed intolerable. A majority of the beedi workers go to private clinics to get medical treatment. It will be helpful to us if the government starts another dispensary in this town with adequate number of doctors and medical staff.

Beedi Workers' Welfare Fund dispensary should opened its braches all over the areas where there is a concentration of the beediworks. They have to be established atlest within a radius of 3-5 k.ms. These dispensaries need to be equipped in terms of providing them with adequate beds, surgical instruments, medicine and other things required for the treatment of the patients. Unless they are equipped well, they will not be able to save thousands of workers from respiratory diseases. The Community Health Workers should be oriented to the development needs of the working children. A T.B. sanatorium has to be established at Malapalayam and Makkudal for providing better treatment to the T.B. patients. It has to be provided with adequate infrastructural facilities to meet the medical requirements of these patients. A series of health camps may have to be organised workers are highly concentrated. Through these camps, an awareness can be created regarding respiratory diseases among the beedi workers. Door canvassing is an effective step to in helping the workers to resort to preventive measures. In addition to this, provision is to be made for the educational and recreational services of the working children at their work places and homes.

REFERENCE

1. Karunanithi, "Health Risks of Beedi Making", *Social Welfare* 44 (June 1997): 9-11.

7

Conclusion

Child labour is a universal phenomenon which has been existing since ancient times. Children were taken as additional hands for domestic, agricultural or industrial work. They sought gainful occupations for reasons such as acquiring technical knowledge, becoming skilled workers, earning more money at an early stage to relieve poverty and non-implementation of compulsory primary education.

Today child labour is a serious problem in Indian. Every third labourer in India is a child. About three-fourths of the children are employed for low wages for their daily bread. Instead of enjoying love and security from their parents, they live under exploitation. Both parents as well as the employers of child workers have failed to realize various problems faced by these working children. Several thousands of children are put to work from dawn to dusk. They are deprived of their rights to study, play and enjoy childhood. Therefore, by and large, they have lost their childhood. Thus, the acts of sending the children for outside work and putting them to domestic work are equally considered as violation of Human Rights. Child labour has assumed monstrous proportions in India and other developing countries since the economic needs of these countries force the children to work. It is estimated by the International Labour Organisation that a third of Asia's 38 million working children belong to India. The State of Tamil Nadu in India accounts for the maximum number of children engaged in the labour force followed by Assam.

The child workers in India are mainly employed in the unorganised and informal sectors, including cottage industries and tertiary service sectors. They are not the products of neither industrialism nor capitalism but the hapless victims of the persistence of the traditional role of the children as workers. They start working at the age of 5 or 6. It is to be noted that the work participation rate of children is higher in the rural areas than in the urban areas. However, it is reported that more girls than boys are engaged in various types of work. That is, perhaps, the reasons while more rural girls than rural boys are out of schools. About 60 per cent of all rural girls and mostly half of all rural girls between the age of 5 and 9 years, 58 per cent of rural girls and 34 per cent of rural boys between the age of 10 and 14 years were not in schools. Even worst 51 per cent of rural girls and 26 per cent of rural boys between the age of 12 and 14 years had never been to school. These figures are consistent with a rural literacy rate of 53 per cent of girls and 73 per cent of boys. On the whole, India's overall record in educating its children can be summed up by an average statement that about one-half of all rural girls and one-fourth of all rural boys are not in schools. There are compelled to do remunerative as well as non-remunerative work.

In Tamil Nadu, the children are engaged in various jobs agriculture, match and fireworks, beediworks, handloom, hosiery, rag picking, auto workshops, petrol pumps, hotels, restaurants, canteens, tea stalls, brick kilns, households and the like. A majority of them are engaged in organised sectors like matchworks, fireworks, beediworks and hosiery industry. In these sectors, about 20-26 per cent of children are employed.

The beedi industry occupies an important place in terms of its capacity to offer potential employment opportunities to a large number of people. It is mainly a cottage and home based industry. It is the job of several thousands of households in Tamil Nadu, Andhra Pradesh, Karnataka and West Bengal. A great majority of the girls and women are engaged in this work. They get raw material from the contractors and making beedis at home. The completed beedis are then handed over to their contractors. In Tamil Nadu, the child labourers engaged in the beediworks are more in, Tirunelveli, Tiruchirapalli and Vellore Districts than in the other districts. The plight of girls engaged n the work is rather miserable. At present, the female children are imparted the skill of beedi making with the purpose of earning for the livelihood of their family and their own marriage. Besides, the acquisition of such a skill is considered an eligibility norm for prospective brides in Tirunelveli District. But, for the boys the beediworks remains a matter of choice in many families. In most cases, the girl children are compelled to take up the work.

The present study is based on the child workers who are predominantly home based in the age group of 5-14 years, in Tirunelveli district of Tamil Nadu. This study explains their socio-demographic profile such as sex, age, religion, education, the size of the family, income, rural-urban background and years of experience. It also deals with exploitation, legal aspects and health problems of the child workers. For the study, a sample of 500 child workers were drawn from the Melapalayam town (125), Keelapavoor block (100), Pappakudi block (85), Kadayam block (75), Alangulam block (65) and Tenkasi block (50) on basis of judgment sampling method. The total sample of 500 consist of, 360 (72 per cent) rural child workers and 140 (28 per cent) urban child workers. The rural child workers comprise 14 boys and 346 girls and urban child workers consist of 16 boys and 124 girls. These workers were selected from 81 areas in five blocks and the town; Melapalayam. The data were collected from the child workers and their parents by administering an interview-scheduled. In addition to this, observation and case study methods were also used to collect data. In addition to the primary data, secondary data were collected from concerned Ministries of Central and State governments, Labour Institute, UNICEF office, ILO office, university libraries and Navajeevan Trust, a voluntary service organisation working for the abolition of child labour in Tirunelveli Dsitrict.

The study discloses that 94 per cent of girls are employed in the beediworks. The proportion of the working girls is fifteen times as much as that of the working boys. Among the rural as well as urban child workers, about 90 per cent girls do this work. Most of the parents do not compel their boys to do this work even if they are unwilling to go to school. They want their boys to secure better jobs with a higher income than the beediworks. In case their songs are not able to secure jobs, they want them to remain unemployed rather than do the beediworks. But, they compel their girls to take up this work as part-time or full-time job in order to supplement their family income and also save money for their marriage. A large majority of the girls at the age of 14 and above 14 years shoulder the responsibility of collecting raw material, making beedis and giving the completed beedis to the contractors. While doing so, in certain situations, some girls are subject to blandishment.

It is observed that in most of the families engaged in the beediworks, indebtedness is a pressing problem which demands child labour and perpetuates it. The situation forces the parents who are under the pressure of indebtedness, to put their children to work compulsorily to supplement their family income for two main reasons. The first reason is to pay interest regularly and the second reason being the sustenance of livelihood of the family members. It is found out that a great majority of rural (80.28 per cent) and urban (77.86 per cent) children do the work mainly due to their parents' pressure to generate more income for these reasons. Besides, acquiring the skill in this work is considered an eligibility criterion for girls to get married without problems.

It is found that there is no significant difference between the average age of rural (11.4 years) and urban (11.14 years) children. Normally at this age they start doing the work. This shows that the children are not given the opportunity to get education even upto primary level. The nation among the parents that earning is better than learning, very much contributes to this state of affairs. Besides, the children find that the school are uninteresting. Many of the schools are housed in dilapidating buildings and managed by one or two teachers. They also find that, in such circumstances, the schools will not be of much useful for the pursuit of knowledge. This may perhaps be an important reasons that they fall back on their family occupation, their *Swadharama*. Their parents consider that this practice, rather than education, has after all the sanctity of tradition.

The study reveals that a great majority of Hindu child workers are engaged in the beediworks in the areas surveyed except the Malapalayam town. Of the rural child workers, 90 per cent of them are Hindus, 6.67 per cent of them are Christians and 3.33 per cent of them are Muslims. Out of the total urban child workers, 16.43 per cent of them are Hindus, 0.72 per cent of them are Christians and 82.86 per cent of them are Muslims. In most of the households, women and their girls are the main bread winners irrespective of their caste and religion. In Christian families, only limited children do this work because, the parents encouraged them to pursue studies besides they get financial support from Fellow Christians.

The analysis of data discloses that the proportion of illiterate child workers in the urban areas (16.43 per cent) is more than the proportion of their rural counterparts (11.94 per cent). More urban than rural parents put their children to work after completing primary education. More girls than boys have studies upto primary level. But, at middle and high school levels, more boys than girls had education. On the other hand, a majority of the girls (65.74 per cent) pursue their studies upto primary level. Inspite of the availability of educational facilities in the Melapalayam town, the children are not able to study upto middle school level because beedi making is main source of their family income.

The main reasons for dropping out of school is that the children are not given chance to pursue their studies. Since they start working to acquire the skill in this work at the age of 7 years, they are assigned to make the required number of beedis everyday. However, a majority of the children like to continue the studies. Some children are not interested in studies because, the primary schools are unable to attract the children. This mainly owes to the lack of infrastructural facilities in the schools and irresponsibility of the teachers. Children are not motivated and encouraged by their teachers. Instead they are treated unkindly. Therefore, there arises a need for facilitating the primary schools in order to promote the quality of education.

Dropouts and illiterate children have to be motivated and encouraged to pursue their studies with an interest. Modern teaching aids like television, over-head projector or colour stills can be used for encouraging the students. A life oriented education is to be implemented instead of the conventional type of education. Young and motivated teachers should be appointed to cater to the educational needs of the children. Thus, the major task of the government is to provide the schools with infrastructural facilities in order to draw the attention of children. Moreover, the government should implement compulsory primary education through a stringent law so that it will put an end to child labour. Besides the efforts on the part of the government, the political parties, trade unions, socio-religious movements and voluntary service organisations should come forward to pressurize the administrators to pay more attention on this issue. It is very much possible to eradicate this problem if politicians and government bureaucrats decide to fight against it with sustained efforts.

The study reports that there is no significant difference between rural and urban child workers with regard to their household size. The average size of the households in rural areas is 6.14 and it is 6.23 in the urban area.

The work efficiency of child workers can be measured in terms of their output per day. They work efficiency of the urban children is relatively more than the work efficiency of the rural children. However, the boys are more efficient than girls in this regard. Girl children are compelled to produce atleast 1,000 beedis per day. If they are not able to touch the limit, they are punished mercilessly. If they complete the target, they are provided with non-vegetarian food atleast once a week. In addition to this, they are also provided with pocket money to spend on their own. If there is a shortage in making beedis, they borrow required beedis from professional lenders. For that, they have to pay interest, which is called Vatti Beedis. This practice is widely prevalent in the areas studied. The average monthly income of rural child workers is Rs. 286.11, but the average monthly income of urban child workers is Rs. 312.86, and the average monthly income of boys and girls is Rs. 246.72 and Rs. 316.27 respectively.

Child workers make beedis at their homes or their neighbours' home. More urban girls than their rural counterparts work in their neighbourhood. Both in rural and urban areas, a great majority of the boys (86.67 per cent) work at their homes. Normally they work for 10-12 hours per day to complete the prescribed number of beedis. The completion of target depends on their experience in the work. It is found out that the children's average years of service in the work is 4.23 in rural areas and 4.38 years in the urban area. The proportion of the urban children's length of experience in this work is more than among their rural counterparts. Especially, the girls are more experienced in the work than the boys. The reason is that the girls start making beedis earlier than the boys.

By and large, the mothers are engaged in the work with their children, for hours together. But, a great majority of the fathers do not do so, but attend to agricultural operations and other works. Since most of the jobs they do are seasonal in nature, they remain unemployed for atleast half the period in a years. Therefore, they want their children to share the responsibility of earning and maintaining their family. This is, one way or other, an exploitation of children for economic reasons. In addition to this work, above 90 per cent of the children assist their parents in household chores irrespective of sex and background. It is thus evident that the parents extract work from their children not only to make beedis but also to assist in household work.

An overwhelming majority (90 per cent) of rural as well as urban children do not like to make beedis because this work prevents them from pursing their studies. Over one-fourth of the rural and urban children do not like the work because it is painful. A majority of the children are every much interested in studies rather than making beedis. But, they are helpless not only in this regard but also in losing all the pleasures of childhood.

Moreover, the child workers especially, girls are subject to harassment by their parents and the contractors. When the girls are not able to complete the prescribed number of beedis per day, they are scolded, sometimes beaten by their parents. As a result of this, they have started borrowing Vatti Beedis from the other beedi labourers in their neighbouring areas or shops which regularly supply beedis to the needy persons with an interest. In addition to this, the girls as directed by their parents, have to handover the finished beedis to the contractors and collect the raw material. While doing so, they are expected to please the contractors against their will; otherwise, the contractors would be rather severe in dealing with them. Sometimes, they supply poor quality raw material and discard several beedis as defective. So, about 90 per cent of the working children are not willing to continue this work. However, they prefer to do some other work to earn money for the sustenance of their family. For instance, 40 per cent of the girls are willing to become teachers, 26.67 per cent of boys are willing to go for self employment and a similar proportion of boys (26.67 per cent) are willing to acquire technical skill. Both in rural and urban areas, about three-fourths of the children are not willing to continue the breediworks. About 90 per cent of the children are punished by their parents for not completing the target. In rural and urban areas, a majority of the children are scolded and beaten for the above reason. Sometimes, they are denied food until they complete their target and not even allowed to play. The contractors also scold the children for not submitting the beedis on time and for not maintaining the quality in making beedis. Girls rather than boys are subject to humiliation, harassment and punishment.

Entertainment in terms of listening to radio, watching cinema, television, visiting fairs, festivals and friends is very much restricted in the case of working children because of their work pressure. Nevertheless, more boys than girls have entertainment. The working children forego their childhood activities and shoulder more family responsibilities. They do not have access to education, play and other entertainment. Their health is affected due to the nature of work. They have stunted growth. The parents make use of their children to produce more and in order to earn more. If they complete the target of a day in advance, they are forced to make additional beedis rather than taking rest or relaxing. They are born as beedi workers, grow as beedi workers and die as beedi workers. They sacrifice their childhood for the sake of their families. They work all day in order to complete the target. In the past, the parents shouldered their family responsibilities with little assistance from their children. But, at present, the children shoulder the major responsibilities with little support from their parents, especially fathers.

Especially, in rural areas, the parents get pass-books in the name of their children by giving false age. So three-fourths of the rural children collect raw material directly from the contractors. But, in the Malapalayam town, a majority of the pass-books are in their parents' name. Therefore, about 57 per cent of the parents collect raw material directly from the contractors. Over 90 per cent of the rural and urban respondents state that they get underweighed and poor quality raw material from the contractors. Sometimes, moistured tobacco dust is supplied.

And the weight decreases considerably after it is dried. Similarly, short, rough and damaged leaves are supplied. Some contractors demand 100 beedis as Commission Beedis or Bodu Vandal (Native usage) for every 1,000 beedis. This is also a major reason for the shortage of raw material. The beedi workers are subject to this sort of exploitation by the contractors.

However, the shortage of raw material is adjusted by purchasing them from the local market. In purchasing raw material every time, the beedi workers of the rural and urban areas incur and average extra expenditure of Rs. 9.6 and Rs. 9.5 respectively. But Rs. 8.9 and Rs. 9.7 are the average expenditure incurred by boys and girls respectively. The girls spend little more than what the boys spend towards the shortage of raw material. Rural child workers spend Rs. 10-14 more towards the purchase of extra raw material than the urban workers.

Nearly three-fourths of the children are aware of various government schemes like minimum wages, scholarship, housing non-formal education, community development, health care and 'Integrated Child Development Programme'. Some of them are also benefited by these schemes.

Over 90 per cent of the parents are found ignorant of the fact that employing children in beediworks is an offence because a majority of them are illiterates. Almost all the beedi workers in the rural areas do not known the laws relating to child labour. But, in urban areas, few parents know it.

The Child Labour (Prohibition and Regulation) Act was passed in 1986. It is totally against the Indian Constitution which states in Article 24 that, "no child below the age of 14 shall be employed to work in any factory or mine or engaged in any other hazardous employment". This Act has to be enforced in such a way as to eliminate child labour altogether. The free and compulsory education for all children until they reach the age of 14 was written into the Constitution not as a right or duty but as a "directive principle". Now it is upto the government to make it as a right in order to tackle the problem. In addition to this, an Act on Compulsory Primary Education has to be introduced in a stringent way to eradicate the problem. The Tamil Nadu Compulsory Primary Education Act, 1994 passed by the State Assembly will come into force after getting approval from the President of India.

More employment opportunities and income generating avenues for adults and parents are to be provided. The families where there is child labour shared to be made accessible to all development programmes and anti-poverty schemes. There should be adequate budgetary allocation for compulsory education by the Sate and Central Governments for the abolition of child labour. It should be monitored by a committee comprising government officials, school teachers, Panchayat authorities, village representatives and voluntary organisations.

According to Section 26 of the Beedi and Cigar Workers' Act 1966, the beedi company should give leave wages on the basis of work done. But, contractors pay only 50-90 per cent of wages. But, they get acknowledgement from them for the whole amount. Some other companies do not pay leave wages, but get the acknowledgement from the workers. If the principal employer deals with the workers directly, the provident found accounts would normally be maintained. But, when it is done by the contractors, only some of them maintain the accounts. Some other contractors would deduct the amount promptly but it would not be deposited in the workers' accounts.

The long hours of work would affect the health of the beedi workers. They are affected by diseases like tuberculosis, choronic bronchitis, nutritional anaemia, back pain, head-ache and eye irritation. It has its adverse effect on the physical devlopment and general health condition of the children. The work pressure makes them weak and stunts their growth. Their physical growth is not directly proportionate to their age. Since the children have the problem of malnutrition, they are highly susceptible to respiratory infections. Three-fourths of the children are affected by respiratory infections because they get exposed to the tobacco dust and tendu leaves for most of the time in a day. Children are suffering from back pain and head-ache because they sit and work for hours together in a particular posture. More members are accommodated in small houses which are poorly ventilated and unghygienically maintained. Ultimately, it leads to serious healthy problems.

A great majority of girls (93.33 per cent) and boys (85.53 per cent) are suffering from respiratory diseases such as chronic cough and tuberculosis. They are also affected by worm infection due to poor hygiene and insanitary conditions prevailing in the residential areas. Due to busy work, they are not able to clean their homes regularly. The problem of nutritional anaemia reduces their weight. Thus, they do not register physical growth in accordance with their age.

The dietary system of the beedi workers reveals that they take full meals only once a day. Usually, they depend on the ordinary rice food and cheap vegetables. In order to encourage the children to complete the prescribed quota per day, the parents provide their children with non-vegetarian food once a week to encourage them to do the work regularly. It clearly indicates that they exploit their children by giving them an incentive in terms of non-vegetarian food. Their food system lacks nutritional value. Therefore, malnutrition is a common problem among the beedi workers.

About three-fourths of the beedi workers prefer private clinics for their treatment rather than visiting the Beedi Workers' Welfare Fund Dispensaries. The reason is that such dispensaries are overcrowded and located in far off places. Therefore, they should be established within a radius of 3-5 k.m.s. It should meet the medical requirements of patients. Community health workers should be acquainted with the development needs of the working children. A TB sanatorium should be set up in the concentrated areas of beediworks like Mukkudal and Melapalayam. The children suffering from respiratory diseases should be identified and treated in the initial stage. Medical camps also should be organised and health awareness should be created among the beedi workers with the help of non-governmental organisations and other organisations.

From these findings, it is evident that as child labour is considered a serious problem, it is to be abolished. Furthermore, no civilised nation on the earth can bear with the employment of child labourers in various occupations. It is paradoxical that the country has made remarkable progress in the economic development and prepares itself to enter the 21st century, but still it has the problem of child labour. It is to be noted that the Constitution of India and several other statutes of the government oppose child labour and plead for the abolition of this evil. It is time for both the Central and State Governments to work together meticulously to eradicate this evil.

While suggesting viable strategies to eradicate child labour from India, the following measures would be taken into consideration:

(i) Enacting a stringent Act relating to compulsory primary education is an effective measure to put an end to this problem. In addition to this, the primary schools across the country should be provided with infrastructural facilities. The quality of primary education would be improved by appointing young and motivated teachers. This has to go with the implementation of modern methods of teaching to attract the children so that they will be interested in pursuing the studies atleast upto middle school. Therefore, the eradication of child labour has to go with compulsory primary education. The local panchayat should be given the responsibility of making cent per cent enrollment

in the primary schools. The developing countries such as Indonesia, Sri Lanka, South Korea and Taiwan have made education compulsory. A few other countries like Algeria, Kenya, Tanzania, Zambia, Malaysia, Philippines and Thailand have aggressively implemented policies relating to universalize the primary education and make a high retention rate. India can also follow a similar type of strategy to eradicate child labour.

(ii) Creating awareness among beedi workers and people about the plight of children engaged in beedi making, is also an important measure to counter the problem of child labour. In this regard, the voluntary service organisations, the National Social Service Schemes of various colleges and universities and other social and religious organisations should come forward to sensitise the people to combat this social menace. This can be done by street plays, film shows, campaigns and rallies. A series of awareness campaigns that would also bring about positive changes among the people, should be organised by the government as well as non-governmental organisations. To put it in a nutshell, it should be a joint venture so that this problem would be tackled as a whole.

(iii) Income generation and creating more employment opportunities for the families engaged in beedi making are also suitable measures to counter the problem. In order to generate income, the families employing children in beediworks, should be given loans with subsidies under Integrated Rural Development Programmes or Self Employment Schemes to start a business or a dairy farm by buying milch cows. It is, indeed, a profitable business that would boost up their family income. In the absence of employment in their own areas,

the heads of household should prepare to seek employment in neighbouring areas and even in far off places to sustain the livelihood of their family. The parents should be prepared to sacrifice their life for the betterment of their children. If they do so, their children would be successful in securing better jobs. Consequently, the forthcoming generations would get rid of this baneful practice.

It is to be noted that these measures, if implemented effectively, would yield the desired results. To achieve this, the entire nation should pay concerted efforts to tide over the problem not wholly, but atleast in a phased manner. No civilised nation on earth can bear with the plight of millions of children toiling themselves not only for their survival but also to sustain the livelihood of their family. It is paradoxical to note that India which has made remarkable progress in science and technology, but, has allowed this problem to take monstrous shapes. Therefore, it is the need of the hour to fight against child labour with a determination to root out this social evil.

Bibliography

BOOKS

Ahmed Shan, Nazir *Child Labour in India*. New Delhi: Anmol Publications, 1992.

Alec Fyfe. *Child Labour*. U.S.A.: Policy Press, 1989.

Burra, Neera. *Born to work*. Bombay: Oxford University Press, 1995.

Chakravarthy, B. *Educational and Child Labour*. Allahabad: Chugh Publications, 1989

Das, Rijani Kanta. *Child Labour in India*. Geneva: International Labour Organisation Press, 1934.

Giri, V.V. *Labour Problem in Indian Industry*. New Delhi: Asian Publishing House, 1960.

Gupta, Manju and Voll, Klaus. *Young Hand at Work:Child Labour in India*. Delhi: Atma Ram & Sons, 1987.

Hirwany, Indira. Cottya, Jacqui aqnd Pandya Pushkar. *Towards Eradication of Child Labour: An International View*. New Delhi: Oxford & IBH Publishing Co. Pvt. Ltd., 1991.

Jain, Mahaveer. *Child Labour in the Gem Polishing Industry in Jaipur*. Noida, Child Labour Cell, National Labour Institute, 1991.

Jain, Mahaveer. *Elimination of Child Labour in India*. Noida: V.V. Giri National Labour Institute, 1996.

Jo Boyden, Pat Holden. *Children of the Cities*. London: Zed Books Ltd., 1991.

Kanbargi, Ramesh. *Child Labour in the Indian Sub-Continent: Dimensions and Implications*. New Delhi: Sage Publications, 1991.

Kangle, K.P. *The Kautilya Arthasashtra, Part II.* Bombay: University of Bombay, 1963.

Krishna Kumari, M.S. *Child Labour in Bangalore City.* Delhi: P.S.P.C.K. 1985.

Kulshreshtha, J.C. *Child Labour in India.* New Delhi: Ashish Publishing House, 1978.

Mendelievich, Elias. *Children at Work.* Geneva: International Labour Organisation, 1979.

Nangia, Parveen. *Child Labour Cause—Effect Syndrome.* New Delhi: Janak Publishers, 1987.

Pandhu, M.K. *Child Labour in India.* Calcutta: Indian Book Exchange, 1979.

Pati, R.N. *Rehabilitation of Child Labourers in India.* New Delhi: Ashish Publishing House, 1991.

Phillips, W.S.K. *Street Children in India.* Jaipur Rawat Publications, 1994.

Sharma, B.K. and Mittan, Vishaa. *Child Labour and Urban Informal Sector.* New Delhi: Deep & Deep Publications, 1990.

Singh, A.N. *Child Labour in India: Socio-Economic Perspective.* Delhi: Shipra Publications, 1990.

Singh, I.S. *Child Labour.* New Delhi: Oxford & IBH Publishing Co. Pvt. Ltd., 1992.

Singh, Surendra and Verma, R.B.S. *Child Labour in Agriculture.* Lucknow: Print House, 1987.

Sinha, S.K. *Child Labour in Calcutta: A Sociological Study.* Calcutta: N.P. Sale (P) Ltd., 1991.

Srinivasnan, Kamala. *Child Labour—Multi Dimensional Problem.* Delhi: Ajanta Publications, 1993.

Stein, E. and Davids, J. *Labour Problem in America.* New York: Farror and Rinchard Inc., 1940.

Sumangala, M. and Nagarajan, B.N. *Economic of Child Labour and Fertility: Study of Peninsular India.* Delhi: B.R. Publishing Corporation (P) Ltd., 1993.

Varandani, G. *Child Labour and Women Workers.* New Delhi: Ashish Publishing House, 1994.

Weiner, Myron. *The Child and the State in India.* Delhi: Oxford University Press, 1991.

Willam, E. Myers. *Protecting Working Children.* New Jersy: Zed Books Ltd., 1991.

Wood, B. Stephen. *Constitutional Politics in the Progressive era: Child Labour and the Law.* Chicago: The University of Chicago Press, 1968.

JOURNALS

Chattoraj, B.N. and Saxena, Rekha. "Victimisation of Children: An Urgent Need for Effective Measures". *Social Change* 20 (September 1993): 23.

Daniel, J. Christopher "Child Worker has Come to Stay". *Social Welfare* 14 (November 1976): 6.

Dharmalingam, A. "Female Beedi Workers in a South Indian Village", *Economic and Political Weekly* 12 (July 1993): 146.

Hussain, Asfak, "Exploitation of Women and Child Labour in Beedi Industry in Samserganj". *Social Welfare* 34 (January 1987): 9.

Karunanithi, G. "Child Labour in Melapalayam", *Social Welfare* 35 (August 1990): 10-11.

Kothari, Smithu. "Child Labour in Sivakasi". *Economic and Political Weekly* 2 (July 1983): 119.

Mehta, Prayag. "Mortgage Child Labour of Vellore Women Beedi Workers' Tale of Woe". *Mainstream* 22 (January 1993): 15.

Moshin, Nadeen. "Poverty-Breeding Ground of Child Labour". *Mainstream* 18 (February 1980): 29-30.

Murthy, G.K., and Rani, T.J. "Wages of Child Labour". *Yojana* 27 (March 1983): 12-14.

Purushottam, P. "A Profile of Beedi Workers". *Social Change* 24 (September 1983): 18-23

Rudgers, Gerry and Standing, Guy. "Economic Roles of Children: Low Income Countries". *International Labour Review* 20 (January-February 1981): 12.

Sahoo, U.C. "Agrarian Dynamics and Child Labour". *Mainstream* 22, (September 1989): 25-26.

Sahoo, U.C. "Child Labour in Surat Textile Industry". *Social Change* 20 (September 1993): 36-37.

Sathyamurthy, T.V. "Children's Work". *Economic and Political Weekly* 30 (April 1995): 807.

Sharma, A.M. "Child Labour in Indian Industries". *Indian Journal of Social Work* 40 (March 1979): 345-252.

Smolowe, J. "The Grim Facts About Child Labour". *Readers Digest,* October 1984.

Srivastava, Sushila and Sheriff, H. "Child Labour in Madras and Vellore" *Social Welfare* 38 (September 1991): 14-17.

Videk Jan. "World's Working Children: Need Protection against Exploitation". *Eastern Economist* 18 (October 1978): 822-823.

MAGAZINES

Anna Davin. "Child Labour: The Working Class Family and Domestic Ideology in 19th Century Britain". *Development and Change,* November 1982.

Burke, Peter. "The Child in the World of Yesterday". *Ekistics:" The Problem and Science of Human Settlement,* September-October 1978.

Chawdhury, Neerja. "Beedi Makers in Madhya Pradesh". *Hindustan Weekly,* August 1980.

Kusan, S. "Poverty—Main Cause of Children Employment". *Lok Kalyan,* January, 1990.

Sadu, A.N. and Singh, Amerjit. "Child Labour in India". *The Indian Worker.* October 1980.

Sandor Komoloski. "Changes in Hungarian Families". *Ekistics: The Problem and Science of Human Settlements,* September-October 1978.

REPORTS

Gurupathasamy. *Report an Child Labour.* New Delhi: Ministry of Labour, [1979].

Karunanithi, G. *Report of Assessment of the Status of Primary Education in Selected Blocks of Kamarajar and V.O.C. Districts of Tamil Nadu.* Madras: United Nations Children Education Fund, [1993].

Karunanithi, G. *Report on Child Labour in North Arcot Ambedkar District: An in-depth Study in Pledged Children in Beediworks.* New Delhi: Indian Council of Social Science Research, [1993].

Karunanithi, G. *Report on Child Labour in Beedi Industry in Tirunelveli-Kattabomman District of Tamil Nadu.* New Delhi: Ministry of Labour. [1995].

Karunanithi, G. *zReport on A Status of Primary—Middle School of Education and Child Labour in Two Blocks in Tirunelveli District of Tamil Nadu.* Tirunelveli: Manonmaniam Sundaranar University, [1997].

Mandakini, Khandekar. *A Report on the Situation of Children and Youth in Greater Bombay.* Bombay: Tata Institute of Social Sciences, [1970].

Mishra, G.P., and Pande P.N. *A Study on Child Labour in Glass Industry, Ferozabad.* New Delhi: Indian Council of Social Science Research, [1992].

Triparhy, Surjyanarayan. *Socio-Economic Problems of Child Labour in A Tribal District of Orissa.* New Delhi: Indian Council of Social Science Research, [1989].

Vidyasagar, R. *A Status Report on Child Labour in Tamil Nadu.* Madras: United Nations Children Education fund. [1995].

Index